Python for Beginners

A Step-by-Step Guide to Learn Python from Zero in just 5 Days

Includes Hands-on-Projects and Exercises

Table of Contents

Introduction

Python is one of the most common programming languages. It is a general-purpose and versatile language. It is powerful as a first language because it is brief and easy to read. Additionally, it is a great language to have in any programmer's stack because it can be used to build many different things.
Python is less complex than other languages such as Java or C++. It is a powerful language and that is why big companies like Yahoo, Red Hat and Google use it.

Enhance your resume by learning to code with Python. This language was created to pave the way to write code that is easy to understand. Although Python has the same basic format as other languages, it provides additional functionality that simplifies life as a programmer.

This book will teach you how to develop basic programming structures, including loops. Then you will move on to expressions, variables, and operators. You will also explore unique data structures such as tuples. You will also learn how to create various python programs using loops and control statements. Additionally, you will also learn how to manipulate data, use of break, and continue statement. The explanation of topics is accompanied by different examples and attempts to emphasize good Python programming practices. We hope that you will enjoy reading and learn new Python concepts.

Chapter 1: Introduction to Python

Python is a multi-purpose language created by Guido van Rossum. The language boasts of a simple syntax that makes it easy for a new learner to understand and use. This chapter will introduce the basics of the Python language. Stay tuned.

Let's get started!

Python is described as a general-purpose language. It has many applications and therefore, you can use it to accomplish many different functions.

The syntax of a python language is clean and the length of the code is short. Developers who have used Python at one point of their lives will express how fun it was to code with Python. The beauty of Python is that it offers you a chance to think more about the task at hand instead of the language syntax.

Some history of Python

The design of the Python language started back in the 1980s and it was first launched in February 1991.

Why was Python developed?

The reason why Guido Van Rossum embarked on the move to design a new programming language is that he wanted a language that could offer a simple syntax just like the ABC. This motivation led to the development of a new language named Python.

But you may be wondering why just the name Python?

First, this language wasn't named after the huge snake called python. No! One of the interests of Rossum was watching comedy. He was a great fan of the comedy series in the late seventies. As a result, the name of the language was borrowed from the "Monty Python's Flying Circus."

Properties of Python

- **Easy to learn** – The syntax of Python is simple and beautiful. Additionally, Python programmers enjoy writing its syntax than other languages. Python simplifies the art of programming and allows the developer to concentrate on the solution instead of the syntax. For a newbie, this is a great choice to start your Python career.

- **Portability** – When it comes to Python portability, it offers you the ability to run Python on different platforms without making any changes.

- **Python is described as a high-level language** – In other words, you don't need to be scared of tedious tasks such as memory management and so on. Alternatively, whenever you execute a Python code, it will automatically change the language to a language that your computer understands. No need to be worried about any lower-level operations.

- **Object-oriented** – Since it is an object-oriented language, it will allow you to compute solutions for the most difficult problems. Object-Oriented Programming makes it possible to divide a large problem into smaller parts by building objects.

- **Has a huge standard library to compute common tasks** – Python has different standard libraries for the programmer to use. As a result, you will not write all the lines of code yourself. Instead, you will only import the library of the relevant code.

A Brief Application of Python

Web Applications

You develop a scalable Web application using CMS and frameworks that are created on Python. Popular environments for developing web applications include Pyramid, Django, Django CMS, and Phone.

Other popular websites like Instagram, Mozilla, and Reddit are written in Python language.

Scientific and Numeric Calculations

There are different Python libraries designed for Scientific and numeric calculations. Libraries such as Numpy and Scipy use Python for general computing purpose. And, there are specially designed libraries like AstroPy for Astronomy, and so on.

Additionally, the Python language is highly applied in data mining, machine learning, and deep learning.

A great Language for Tech Programmers

The Python language is an important tool used to demonstrate programming to newbies and children. It is a great language that has important capabilities and features. However, it is one of the easiest languages to learn because it has a simple syntax.

Building Software Prototypes

Compared to Java and C++, Python is a bit slow. It may not be a great choice when resources are restricted and efficiency is made compulsory.

But Python is a powerful language to build prototypes. For instance: You can apply the Pygame library to develop the prototype of your game first. If you enjoy the prototype, you can decide to use C++ to develop the actual game.

Why you should select Python as your Language

Simple, Beautiful Syntax

Let no one deceive you; it is fun to program in Python. It is easier to understand a line of code and write a Python code. The syntax looks natural. For example:

```
b = 4

c = 3

sum = b + c

Print (sum)
```

Even if it is your first time to program, you can manage to guess the function of this simple program.

Not a Very Strict Language

No need to define the type of variable in Python language. More so, you don't need to end a line with a semicolon. However, Python demands that you adhere to good practices like the right indentation. These little things simplify learning Python for beginners.

The Language is Expressive

Python will let you write powerful programs that have many functions using fewer lines of code. Once you start to write your own programs, you will be surprised at how much you can do with Python language.

Lovely Community and Support

There is a large community of Python developers. You will come across different active online forums, which can be helpful while learning how to program in Python.

Reasons you should consider to write Software Applications using Python

Easy to Read and Maintain

While creating an application, you need to concentrate on the brilliant nature of the source code to make the process of updating and maintaining the code easy. The Python Syntax permits you to demonstrate concepts without writing extra code.

Besides this, Python provides the chance to use English terms instead of punctuations. For that reason, one can use Python to build custom applications without writing extra code. When you write code that is easy to read, it simplifies the process of updating the software.

Compatible with Key Platforms and Systems

As said before, Python can run in different operating systems. You can even decide to use Python Interprets to run the code on a defined platform. Additionally, Python is an interpreted programming language. In other words, you can run the same piece of code on different platforms without recompiling. Therefore, you don't need to recompile the code once you make any changes. In fact, you can run the altered code without recompiling and confirm the effect of changes done to the code instantly. This feature allows developers to change the code without increasing the building time.

Many Open Source Technologies and Frameworks

Since Python is an open source language, it helps save the cost of the software. Why? You can include different open source Python frameworks, development tools, and libraries to reduce the development time without increasing the cost of development.

Breakdown the Intricate Software Development

You can use Python to build both web and desktop applications. Still, you can use it to develop complex scientific programs. Python is designed with properties to support data analysis and visualization. You can use the data analysis properties of Python to build big custom solutions without spending extra energy and time. Alternatively, the data libraries and visualizations provided by Python language allow you to visualize and present data in a friendly and effective way.

Apply Test Driven Development (TDD)

With Python, it is possible to develop a software prototype application very fast. Furthermore, the software application can be developed directly from the prototype by refactoring the python code.

Still, Python simplifies coding and testing through the use of TDD methodology. You can quickly write the relevant tests before writing code and adopting the tests to examine the application code. Also, the tests can help confirm whether the application fulfills predefined requirements depending on the source code.

However, Python has its own drawbacks. For example, it doesn't have built-in features available in other modern programming languages. As a result, you just need to use Python libraries and frameworks to increase custom software development. Also, Python is slower than other languages like Java and C++. This means you will need to boost the Python application by implementing changes to the application code. But still, you can use Python to simplify software maintenance and speed up the process of software development.

Chapter 2: How to Install Python

In this chapter, you will learn how to install Python on your Windows computer, Linux, and Mac OS X.

How to Install Python in Mac OS X

1. Navigate to the Python Download page on the official website and click "Download Python" (There will be a version name at the end.)

2. Once the download completes, open the package and begin to follow the instructions. You will then see the notification "The installation was successful" when Python completes the installation successfully.

3. It is advised to download a great text editor before you can start the installation process. For new beginners, you should download the Sublime Text. It is available for free.

4. The installation process of Sublime text is quite simple. You only need to run the Sublime Text Disk Image file you download and follow the instructions.

5. Once the installation is over, open the Sublime Text and navigate to File > New File. Next, save the file using the .py extension such as beginner.py or hello.py.

6. Write the code and save it. For newbies, here's a code to use:

   Print ("Hello, World!")

The simple program prints, "Hello, World!"

7. Navigate to Tool > Build. Here, you can move to the bottom to see the results of your program.

Install and Run Python in Linux

1. First, you need to install the dependencies below.

```
$ sudo apt-get install build-essential checkinstall
$ sudo apt-get install libreadline-gplv2-dev libncursesw5-dev libssl-dev
libsqlite3-dev tk-dev libgdbm-dev libc6-dev libbz2-dev
```

2. Navigate to the Download Python page located on the official site and click "Download Python 3.6.0". If you see a different version, don't hesitate to download it.

3. Go to the terminal and locate the path where the file is downloaded and execute the following command:

   $ tar -xvf Python-3.6.0.tgz

This line will remove your zipped file. Just know that the filename will be different if you downloaded a different version. So you should ensure you use the right filename.

4. Now shift to the extracted directory.

```
$ cd Python-3.6.0
```

5. Use these commands to compile Python source code on your OS.

```
$ ./configure
$ make
$ make install
```

6. It is advised that you install Sublime Text if you are a new beginner. If you are using Ubuntu, then you should run the following commands to install Sublime Text:

```
$ sudo add-apt-repository -y ppa:webupd8team/sublime-text-2
$ sudo apt-get update
$ sudo apt-get install sublime-text
```

7. Now open Sublime text. To build a new file, navigate to File>New File

8. Save the file using the .py file extension such as beginner.py

9. Write the code and save it. For beginners, you can use the following code:

   Print ("Where are you?")

   This program will display, "Where are you?"

10. Navigate to the Tool > Build. You can view the output at the bottom of the Sublime Text.

Install Python in Windows

1. Navigate to the Download Python page found on the official site and click on the Download Python 3.6.0.

2. Once the download is complete, open the file and start the installation process. Once the installation of Python is done, IDLE is installed alongside.

3. Open the IDLE, paste the code below and press enter.

   Print ("Hello, World!")

4. To develop a file in IDLE, navigate to the File > New Window.

5. Write a Python code and save it with a .py file extension.

6. Navigate to the Run > Run module and view the output.

Python Interaction

As said in the first chapter, the Python language is popular because of the level of flexibility and dynamic that a developer can use to achieve different things. For example, you can use Python interactively when you want to test a statement on a line-by-line basis or when you are trying to learn new properties. You can also use it in script mode when you have a whole file of statements that you want to interpret.

Python has the Command Line Window or the IDLE that allow programmers to use it interactively.

Let's look at the command line interaction

The command line is the simplest way for one to work with Python. With this tool, one can visualize the way Python works as it responds to every finished typed command. It might not be the best tool to use to interact with Python but still is the easiest means to use to learn how Python works.

How to start Python

There are different methods that you can use to access the command line of Python depending on the type of operating system running in your computer:

- For Windows users, they can start the Python command line by clicking on the menu item found on the Start menu. Also, users of Windows can navigate to the folder that has a shortcut and click on the Python command line.

- For those using Linux and Mac OS systems, you need to run the Terminal Tool and type the Python command to start a session.

Computer commands are used to instruct the machine on what to do. Therefore, if you want Python to perform a given task, you have to type commands that it will interpret. Next, Python will translate the commands to instructions which the machine is familiar with and execute.

To understand how Python works, you will use the print command to print a simple message: Welcome to Python.

1. First, open your Python command line tool.
2. Then type the following code at the >>> prompt

   Print ("Welcome to Python!")

3. Now press enter to instruct Python that you are done writing the command.
4. Next, you will see the message Welcome to Python! On the command line window.

In the above example, Python responded the right way because you typed the correct command in the right format. Let's say you typed the command incorrectly; then Python will have responded with the following message: Syntax error: Invalid syntax.

When you come across a syntax error message, then know that you have entered an incomplete statement in your code. For example, typing the keyword print in the capital letter will result in a syntax error.

When you are programming with Python, it gives you room to do away with the print command completely by only typing your statements within quotes. For example: “Welcome to Python!”

How to exit from Python

Once you are done using Python, you can exit by typing the following commands:

Quit ()

Exit ()

Control-Z then press Enter

IDLE: Python’s Integrated Development Environment

The IDLE is part of Python’s installation package but you can decide to download more complex third-party IDEs. The IDLE tool delivers a stable platform for one to write code and work interactively with Python. You can find IDLE in the same folder the command line Icon is located. Once you click the IDLE icon, it will direct you to the Python Shell Window.

When you first open the IDLE, it will start in the Shell. The shell is an interactive window for you to type in Python code and monitor the output in the same window.

Note: On windows, when you click a Python file on the desktop, the Windows system will run the program. However, if you right click on the file, there would be an option for the Edit with IDLE. To modify an existing Python file, open the IDLE, and then open the file via the File menu.

First Python Program

Up until now, you have already written the first program in Python. The "Hello World Program" is always the first program to write in any programming language.

In the following example, we shall look at a different type of program. To start, open the IDLE and create a new window. If you don't know how to create a new window, just click on "New Window located under the File Menu". Then you can type the following program:

```
temp = eval(input('Enter a temperature in Celsius: '))
print('In Fahrenheit, that is', 9/5*temp+32)
```

Navigate to the Run menu of the IDLE and select the Run Module. If you don't want to do so, just press F5. The IDLE will request you to save the file and you should proceed and so. Make sure you append .py to the filename because the IDLE will not automatically do so. The .py extension will tell the IDLE the file type is for Python and thus include colors to make the program easier to read.

Once you save the program, it will be executed in the shell window. The program will request you for a temperature. Type the value 20 and click Enter. The output of the program will be like this:

```
Enter a temperature in Celsius: 20
In Fahrenheit, that is 68.0
```

Let's see how the program works. The first line requests the user to type the temperature. The role of the input function is to prompt the user to enter something and to store what the user types. The part enclosed in quotes is what the user sees. This is referred to as a "string" and it will appear to the user of the program exactly as it is in the code itself. The "eval" is a function but you won't understand until when we shall look at python functions. So for now, just know that it is used when we want to get numerical input.

The next program you will learn is one that calculates the average of two numbers entered by the user.

```
num1 = eval(input('Enter the first number: '))
num2 = eval(input('Enter the second number: '))
print('The average of the numbers you entered is', (num1+num2)/2)
```

Python language has a great feature known as line indentation. Python applies the following feature on things that you will learn soon. On the flipside, spaces in other places aren't really important. For example, these lines have the same effect:

```
print('Hello world!')
print ('Hello world!')
print( 'Hello world!' )
```

In general, computers will only run depending on the command you type and they always interpret things literally.

On the other hand, Python operates based on the placement of commas and parentheses so that it can know what's what. It is not a great language to predict whatever you mean so you will need to be accurate. At first, it will sound frustrating to get all commas and parentheses in the correct places but after some time, it will be more natural. Even when you program for a long time, you will still forget something. Luckily, the Python interpreter helps show you areas where you have made mistakes.

Accepting input

The input function is an easy way for your program to receive information from users through the program. For example:

```
name = input('Enter your name: ')
print('Hello, ', name)
```

The standard syntax is:

Variable name = input (message to user)

This structure is used when you want to get a text from a user. However, if you want to get numbers from the user to include in computations, you will have to go an extra mile. Check out this example:

```
num = eval(input('Enter a number: '))
print('Your number squared:', num*num)
```

The “eval” function will change the text typed by the user into a number. One great feature of this is that you can type expressions such as 2*4+ 9 and the “eval” will determine the result for you.

Note: When you run a program and nothing seems to be taking place, press enter. Sometimes, there is always a glitch in IDLE that frequently takes place with input statements.

Printing

Consider the following example:

Print (‘Hello there’)

The function “print” should be enclosed with parenthesis around its arguments. In the following program, the argument is the string ‘Hello there.’ Anything that is enclosed in the quotes will be displayed exactly as it appears. In the first program shown below, it will print ‘4+ 2’ while the second program will print 8.

print (‘4+2’)

print (4+ 4)

To display different things at once, you need to use commas to separate the items. However, Python will automatically insert spaces between the items. For example:

```
print('The value of 3+4 is', 3+4)
print('A', 1, 'XYZ', 2)
```

Output

```
The value of 3+4 is 7
A 1 XYZ 2
```

Chapter 3: Python Numbers

Integers and Decimal Numbers

Computer chips are designed uniquely. Because of that, integers and decimal numbers have a special representation. The most critical thing to recall is that you only get 15 or so digits of accuracy. It would be great if there were no boundary to the precision but computations happen so fast if you remove the numbers at some point.

When it comes to decimal numbers, the last digit can be left off because computers work in binary and the standard system of numbering for humans is to base 10. This means that if you consider the division of 7/3 in the Python shell, it will display 2.333333333335. This type of operation is defined as a round-off error. In scientific and mathematical computations, this can be a big problem.

Math Operators

This list has common Python operators.

```
+ addition
- subtraction
* multiplication
/ division
** exponentiation
// integer division
% modulo (remainder)
```

Integer division: In general, the integer division will work as the usual division for positive numbers except that it removes the decimal part. For example, 8/5 is 1.6, 8//5 equal to 1. You will learn more about the application of the following operator as you continue to learn Python.

Modulo: This operator % displays the remainder result after division. So if you take 5%3, the result will be 2. The modulo operator is useful when you want to determine if a number is divisible. If the number leaves a remainder of 0, then it is said to be divisible. If not, the number is said not to be divisible.

Another application of the module comes in when you want to set a specific feature in a loop to happen often; you can use it to determine the loop variable modulo 2 is equivalent to 0. If yes, then perform a certain action.

The modulo operator is popular in formulas. If you want to "wrap things around" and return to the start, you can use the modulo.

Consider a game of 5 players. Let's say you defined a variable player that will monitor the current player. Once player 5 completes his turn, it is the role of player 1. You can use the modulo operator to handle this operation:

```
player = player%5+1
```

This code means when a player is 5, player%5 will be equal to 0 and return to player 1.

The Order of Operations

The order of operations refers to the steps in the execution of operators. When you have more than two operators, an order of operations has to be followed. In general, exponentiation is executed first, then multiplication, and division. Addition and subtraction are the last. The standard math mnemonic is "PEMDAS, which stands for Please Excuse My Dear Aunt Sally". This can be helpful if you are likely to forget.

This is useful when you want to compute an average. Say, for instance, you have three variables m, n, and y. And you want to determine the average. If you use the expression m+n+y/3, you get a wrong result because the division has higher precedence than addition. Therefore, you need to apply parentheses: (m+n+y)/3.

Note: If you have doubts over something, then proceed and use parentheses. There is no problem when you use parentheses.

Random Numbers

If you want to make your computer game interesting, then you will need to apply the random feature. Python has a module called random. This module will allow you to include random numbers in your program.

First, let's define a module. The Python language comprises of math operations, loops, and functions. All other things are contained in modules. If you need to use a module, you will first need to import. By importing, you will be making Python aware.

Another function is the randint from the random library. Before you can use this function, you will need to write this statement:

```
from random import randint
```

To use the randint function is straightforward: *randint (a, b)* will display a random integer between a and b. For example:

```
from random import randint
x = randint(1,10)
print('A random number between 1 and 10: ', x)

A random number between 1 and 10: 7
```

The random number will be unique every time the program is run.

Functions in Maths

In Python, there is another math module that has familiar math functions such as tan, cos, sqrt, floor, and many more. Also, there is the constants pi, hyperbolic functions, and the inverse trig functions. Check this example:

```
from math import sin, pi
print('Pi is roughly', pi)
print('sin(0) =', sin(0))
Pi is roughly 3.14159265359
sin(0) = 0.0
```

In-built Math Functions

Python has two built-in math functions.

- Abs
- Round

There two arguments for the round function. The first argument represents the number that should be rounded while the second number is the decimal place that you need to round.

Get Assistance from Python

Python has documentation that you can use to get assistance on the math module. For instance, open the Python shell and the type these two commands:

>>> import math

>>> dir(math)

Shell Calculator

The Python shell can be an excellent calculator. Below is a session example:

```
>>> 23**2
529
>>> s = 0
>>> for n in range(1,10001):
s = s + 1/n**2


1.6448340718480652
>>> from math import *
>>> factorial(10)
3628800
```

This example adds the numbers s 1 + 1/4 + 1/9 + ··· + 1/100002.

The output is stored inside a variable. To determine the value of the variable, type the name, and click enter. Examining variables is important to debug your problems. When a program doesn't work correctly, you can type the variable names into the shell once the program is done knowing what the values are.

Practice Exercise

1. Create a program that prints 50 random integers, each between 3-6.

2. Create a program that will print random numbers between 1-10.

3. Write a program that prompts the user to type two numbers, m, and n, and determine the average.

4. Create a program that prompts the user to enter the number of seconds and display the number of minutes and seconds that is.

Chapter 4: Functions

Functions in any programming language are important because they help divide a large program into small sections that are easy to control. Functions are still important if you experience a situation where you write the same code at different points in your program. Python function blocks starts with the keyword **def** followed by the name of the function and parentheses. Any input arguments or parameters should be placed within these parentheses. Still, you can define parameters inside these parentheses.

Why You Need Functions

Functions control inputs and outputs in computer programs. Programming languages have been created to work on data and the functions are the best way to convert this type of data.

In particular, the main code of a program is a function. Every function is logically connected to work from the main code. However, if a function has not been previously defined, you will need to define one before you use it.

So, functions can be said to be tasks that a user wants to conduct. However, defining a function once with a name provides the chance to reuse the functionality without making the main program to appear scary. This will rapidly eliminate the lines of code and make the debugging easier.

You will learn this later, but for now, you need to note that the reason why you use a function is because of the reusability. The fact that complicated operations can be compiled as singular tasks that can run with only a call is the reason why computer codes are clearer.

Each language of programming allows you to create and use the functions to conduct different tasks with a single call. And you can make various calls without getting worried about logically structuring the code into the main code every single moment.

Python Functions

The Python functions are a great example of reusability. This helps serve a wide range of applications right from web development to testing. The Python interpreter has different functions that are available to use. And you can always bring in other libraries to your program that has pre-defined functions already available to use.

All that you need to do is to download the necessary packages and freely provide the relevant functionalities by importing them to your code.

Therefore, once a function is defined, it can be used multiple times at any point of the code. The reason is that Python is by the DRY principle of software engineering. This principle focuses on replacing any repetition of software patterns with abstractions to avoid redundancy and confirm that they can be used freely without showing any features of their implementations.

DRY extends to Don't Repeat Yourself and this particular feature of re-usable blocks of codes is very important for realizing abstraction in Python. Therefore, to apply a function, you only need the name, its arguments, and purpose if it takes any and the type of results if returns any.

It is the same as using an automobile or telephone where you don't need to know the working of its components to use them. Instead, it is already built to provide common purposes that you can directly use to attain your goals and devote your time to implement all innovative features of your application program. And no one really wants to understand the inner operation of a function as long as it does its work.

Therefore, with Python, unless you want to create a new function or change existing works, you don't need to know anything that happens on the inside until it works the way you need it to. It is like a vehicle, where you will be required to understand how it works before you build or fix one. Alternatively, once you create a working function, you can use it repeatedly without the need to look at the contents inside it ever again.

You can call a function as part of a program that is written once and can be run anytime it is needed in the program. This makes the code reusable.

A function is a subprogram that operates on data and generates output.

To define a python function, you need to use the "def" keyword before the name of your function and add parentheses to its end, followed by a colon (:)

Python has indentation to show blocks rather than brackets to improve the readability of codes.

A function in Python may have a different number of parameters or none at all. Therefore, for the moments when you need your function to work on variables from other blocks of code or your main program, it may involve a different number of parameters and generate results.

A python function can still return a value or not. The value can be generated from the function's execution or even an expression or value that you emphasize after the keyword "return". And once a return statement is executed, the program flow returns to the state next to the function call and gets executed from there.

Therefore, to call a Python function at any point in your code, you will only need to use its name and pass arguments in the parentheses, if any.

The rules for defining a function are similar to naming a variable. It starts with either letter from A-Z, a-z in both lower cases, and upper cases, or an underscore (_). The remaining name has underscores (_), digits (0-9), and letters in lowercase or upper case.

1. A reserved keyword might not be selected as an identifier.
2. The right use of grammar to improve the readability of the code.

It is the right practice to name a Python function based on what it achieves. Apply a docstring below the first line of a function declaration. It is a documentation string, and it describes what the function implements.

Basics of Functions

To define functions in Python, you use the def statement. This statement ends with a colon, and the code inside the function is indented just below the def statement. For example:

```
def print_hello():
    print('Hello!')

print_hello()
print('1234567')
print_hello()
```

Let's look at this program in detail.

From the following program, the last part of the code has a function call.

Functions are vital because they help you avoid the need to write the same code everywhere.

If you want to draw a box of stars in your program, a Python function can be helpful. Whenever you want a box, you simply insert the function to draw the box instead of typing different lines of redundant code. Below is the function:

```
def draw_square():
  print('*' * 15)
  print('*', ' '*11, '*')
  print('*', ' '*11, '*')
  print('*' * 15)
```

The advantage this brings is if you want to alter the size of the box, you only need to alter the code inside the function. On the other hand, if you try to copy and paste the box code everywhere, then you will require to change every place you paste it.

Arguments

In most programming languages, one can pass values to functions. For example:

```
def print_hello(n):
 print('Hello ' * n)
 print()

print_hello(3)
print_hello(5)
times = 2
print_hello(times)
```

By calling the print_hello function using the value 3, the value is kept in the variable n. You can then point to this variable within the function's code.

In Python programming, it is possible to pass a different value to the same function.

```
def multiple_print(string, n)
print(string * n)
print()

multiple_print('Hello', 5)
multiple_print('A', 10)
```

Returning values

Programming is an interesting thing to learn, especially when writing functions. Besides just passing values to functions, you can also create functions that return a result after computation is over.

The following example changes the temperature from Celsius to Fahrenheit.

```
def convert(t):
return t*9/5+32
print(convert(20))
```

This program has a return statement that sends the output of a function computation back to the caller. Keep in mind that the function doesn't print anything. The printing happens outside the function.

In this case, you can compute the math with the following result:

```
print(convert(20)+5)
```

The math module in Python has trig functions but the functions only work in radians. Here is a sine function that can work in degrees.

```
from math import pi, sin
def deg_sin(x):
return sin(pi*x/180)
```

A function can still return more than one value as a list.

Types of Python Functions

There are many categories of Python Functions. And each of the functions is unique. Here are different categories of Python functions:

- Python Recursion Functions
- Python Built-in Functions
- Python user-defined functions
- Python lambda functions

Let us dive deep and learn more about these functions.

In-built Python Functions

The python interpreter has different functions available to use. These functions are referred to as built-in functions. For instance, the print () function will display the object to the standard output device or the text stream file.

Python 3.6 has 68 built-in functions. For purposes of simplicity, let us look at the main functions used, and we can start on from there.

Python abs () Function

This function will return the absolute value of any number entered. If the number is complex, abs () displays a magnitude.

Syntax

The general syntax of the abs () function is:

Abs (num)

Parameters

The abs () function accepts a single argument:

- **Num**-This is a number whose absolute value should be returned. This number can be:
    a. Integer
    b. Complex number
    c. Floating number

Example

```
# random integer
integer = -20
print('Absolute value of -20 is:', abs(integer))

#random floating number
floating = -30.33
print('Absolute value of -30.33 is:', abs(floating))
```

Python all () function

The all () function will output True if all elements in a specific iterable are true. If not, it will display False.

Syntax

The syntax of all () method is:

all (iterable)

Parameters

The all () method accepts a single parameter:

- Iterable- Any iterable (tuple, list, dictionary, etc.) which has the elements.

  For example:

```
# all values true
l = [1, 3, 4, 5]
print(all(l))

# all values false
l = [0, False]
print(all(l))

# one false value
l = [1, 3, 4, 0]
print(all(l))

# one true value
l = [0, False, 5]
print(all(l))

# empty iterable
l = []
print(all(l))

Output

True
False
False
False
True
```

Python ascii () Function

This method will return a string with a printable representation of an object. It skips the non-ASCII characters inside the string using u, x, or U escapes.

Syntax

The syntax of the asci () method is:

ascii (object)

Parameters
The asci method accepts objects like list, string, etc.

Example

```
normalText = 'Python is interesting'
print(ascii(normalText))

otherText = 'Pythön is interesting'
print(ascii(otherText))

print('Pythn is interesting')

Output

'Python is interesting'
'Pythn is interesting'
Pythön is interesting
```

Python bin () function

The bin function changes and returns the binary string of a specific integer. In case the parameter is not an integer, it has to execute the _index_ () method to run an integer.

The syntax of a bin () method is: bin (num)

The bin () method accepts a single parameter:

- Num-This is an integer number whose binary equivalent has to be computed. If not an integer, it has to run the _index_ () method to output an integer.

```
number = 5
print('The binary equivalent of 5 is:', bin(number))

Output

The binary equivalent of 5 is: 0b101
```

Python bool () function

The bool () method will change and return the equivalent binary string of a particular integer. If the parameter is not an integer, it has to execute the __index__ () to display an integer.

The syntax of bool () method is:

Bool([value])

Parameters

It is not a must to pass a value to bool (). If you don't pass a value, bool () returns a False value.

Overall, bool () accepts a single parameter value.

Example:

```
test = []
print(test,'is',bool(test))

test = [0]
print(test,'is',bool(test))

test = 0.0
print(test,'is',bool(test))

test = None
print(test,'is',bool(test))

test = True
print(test,'is',bool(test))

test = 'Easy string'
print(test,'is',bool(test))

Output

[] is False
[0] is True
0.0 is False
None is False
True is True
Easy string is True
```

Python Recursive functions

In Python programming, a function can reference another function. Also, functions don't have to be called by other functions, but instead it can call itself.

An example of a recursive function is one to find the factorial of numbers. 6 factorial means 1*2*3*4*5*6= 720

Example:

```
# An example of a recursive function to
# find the factorial of a number

def calc_factorial(x):
    <em>"""This is a recursive function
    to find the factorial of an integer"""

    </em>if x == 1:
        return 1
    else:
        return (x * calc_factorial(x-1))

num = 4
print("The factorial of", num, "is", calc_factorial(num))
```

In this example, calc_factorial () is a recursive function.

Pros recursion

1. A recursive function improves the appearance of code. A code looks elegant and clean.
2. A difficult problem is divided into small parts using recursion

Cons of recursion

1. Recursive calls consume a lot of time and memory.
2. Sometimes the logic of recursion is difficult to follow.

Python Lambda Functions

A function without a name is referred to as an anonymous function. The lambda keyword denotes anonymous.

Using Lambda functions in Python

The syntax of python lambda function includes:

Lambda arguments: expression

Example:

```
# Program to show the use of lambda functions

double = lambda x: x * 2

# Output: 10
print(double(5))

10

In [1]:
```

Python user-defined functions

As the name suggests, user-defined functions refer to functions defined by the user.

Pros of user-defined functions

1. User-defined functions assist in the sub-dividing a huge program into small parts.
2. If there is a repeated code in a program, the function can include codes and execute when required by the calling function.
3. Programmers that work on a big project can divide the workload by computing various functions.

Syntax

```
def function_name(argument1, argument2, ...) :
      statement_1
      statement_2
      ....
```

In summary, the concepts explored in this chapter should help you develop your own Python functions by adding operability and functionality to the same.

This will be useful when you try to build an application by simplifying the process and make it suitable for your personal needs. Now, you need to be able to use Python functions to create applications easily.

Chapter 5: Python Variables

If you plan to write complex code, then you must include data that will change the execution of the program.

That is what you are going to learn in this chapter. At the end of the chapter, you will learn how the abstract object term can explain each section of data in Python and you will learn how to change objects with the help of variables.

Variables in Python programming are the data types in Python as the name implies. In the programming world, variables are memory location where you store a value. The value that you store might change in the future depending on the descriptions.

In Python, a variable is created once a value is assigned to it. It doesn't need any extra commands to declare a variable in Python. There are specific rules and guidelines to adhere while writing a variable.

Assignment of Variable

Look at variables as a name linked to a specific object. In Python programming, you don't need to declare variables before you use like it is in other programming languages. Instead, you assign a value to a variable and begin to use it immediately. The assignment occurs using a single equals sign (=):

Y= 100

The same way a literal value can be shown from the interpreter using a REPL session, so it is to a variable:

Later if you assign a new value to Y and use it again, the new value is replaced.

Still, Python has room for chained assignment. In other words, you can assign the same value to different variables at the same time.

Example:

```
>>> a = b = c = 300
>>> print(a, b, c)
300 300 300
```

This chained assignment allocates 300 to the three variables simultaneously. Most variables in other programming languages are statically typed. This means that a variable is always declared to hold a given data type. Now any value that is assigned to this variable should be similar to the data type of the variable.

However, variables in Python don't follow this pattern. In fact, a variable can hold a value featuring a different data type and later re-assigned to hold another type.

Object References

What really happens when you assign a variable?

This is a vital question in Python programming because it is different from what goes on in other languages.

First, Python is an object-oriented language. In fact, each data item in Python is an object of a given type.

Consider the following example:

```
>>> print(300)
300
```

When the interpreter comes across the statement print (300), the following takes place:

- Assigns it the value 300.
- Builds an integer object.
- Outputs it to the console.

Example

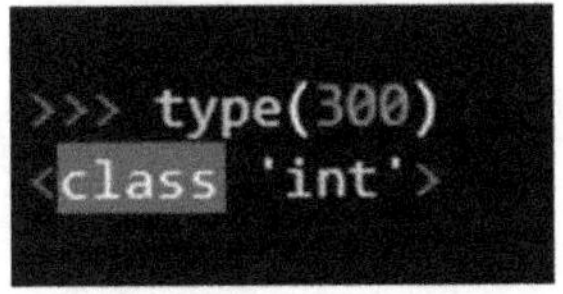

```
>>> type(300)
<class 'int'>
```

Python variables are the symbolic name that can act as a pointer to an object. When an object is allocated a variable, a reference to the object can be done using a name. However, the data itself is contained within the object.

The life of an object starts once it is created; at this point, the object may have one reference. In the lifetime of an object, other references to the object can be created. An object will remain active as long as it has one reference.

But when the number of references to the object drops to zero, it cannot be accessed again. The lifetime of the object is then said to be over. Python will finally realize that it is inaccessible and take the allocated space so that it can be used for something different. This process is called garbage collection.

Object Identity

Every object created in Python is assigned a number to identify it. In other words, there is no point where two objects will share the same identifier during a time when the lifetimes of the object overlap. When the count of an object reference drops to zero and it is garbage collected, then the identifying number of the object is reclaimed to be used again

```
>>> n = 300
>>> m = n
>>> id(n)
60127840
>>> id(m)
60127840

>>> m = 400
>>> id(m)
60127872
```

.

Cache Small Integer Values

From your knowledge of the variable assignment and referencing of variables in Python, you will not be surprised by:

```
>>> m = 300
>>> n = 300
>>> id(m)
60062304
>>> id(n)
60062896
```

In this code, Python defines the object of integer type using the value 300 and allows m to refer to it. Similarly, n is allocated to an integer object using the value 300 but not with a different object. Let us consider the following:

```
>>> m = 30
>>> n = 30
>>> id(m)
1405569120
>>> id(n)
1405569120
```

In this example, both m and n have been separately allocated to integer objects holding the value 30. But in this instance, id (m) and id (n) are similar.

The interpreter will develop objects between [-5, 256] at the start, and later reuse it. Therefore, if you assign unique variables to an integer value, it will point to the same object.

Variable Names

The previous examples have used short variables like m and n. But still, you can create variable names with long words. This really helps to explain the use of the variable when a user sees the variable.

In general, Python variable names can be of any length and can have upper case and lowercase letters. Also, the variable names can include digits from 0-9 and the underscore character. Another restriction is that the first character of a variable cannot be an integer.

For instance, all these are important variable names:

```
>>> name = "Bob"
>>> Age = 54
>>> has_W2 = True
>>> print(name, Age, has_W2)
Bob 54 True
```

Since a variable cannot start with a digit, this program will show the following result:

```
>>> 1099_filed = False
SyntaxError: invalid token
```

Keep in mind too that lowercase letters and uppercase letters are different. Using the underscore character is important as well:

```
>>> age = 1
>>> Age = 2
>>> aGe = 3
>>> AGE = 4
>>> a_g_e = 5
>>> _age = 6
>>> age_ = 7
>>> _AGE_ = 8

>>> print(age, Age, aGe, AGE, a_g_e, _age, age_, _AGE_)
1 2 3 4 5 6 7 8
```

Nothing will prevent you from defining two variables in the same program that have names like number and Number. However, this is not advised at all. It would definitely confuse anyone going through your code, and even yourself, after you have stayed for a while without looking at the code.

It is important to assign descriptive variable names to make it clear on what it is being used for. For instance, say you are determining the number of people who have graduated from college. You may choose any of the following:

```
>>> numberofcollegegraduates = 2500
>>> NUMBEROFCOLLEGEGRADUATES = 2500
>>> numberOfCollegeGraduates = 2500
>>> NumberOfCollegeGraduates = 2500
>>> number_of_college_graduates = 2500

>>> print(numberofcollegegraduates, NUMBEROFCOLLEGEGRADUATES,
... numberOfCollegeGraduates, NumberOfCollegeGraduates,
... number_of_college_graduates)
2500 2500 2500 2500 2500
```

All are great choices than n , or any other variable. At least you can understand from the name the value of the variable.

Reserved Keywords

There is one limit on identifiers names. The Python language has a unique set of keyword that defines specific language functionality. No object can use the same name as a reserved keyword.

Python Keywords

False	def	if	raise
None	del	import	return
True	elif	in	try
and	else	is	while
as	except	lambda	with
assert	finally	nonlocal	yield
break	for	not	
class	from	or	
continue	global	pass	

You can see reserved words in python by typing help ("keywords") on the Python interpreter. Reserved keywords are case-sensitive. So you should never change them but use them exactly as they appear. All of them are in lowercase, except for the following:

True, False, and None.

If you attempt to create a variable using a reserved word, it will result in an error.

Chapter 6: Operators and Expressions

The previous chapter looked at variables in Python. We hope that now you have a good knowledge of defining and naming Python objects.

Let us use them to do some work.

First, we shall start to look at Python operators:

Python operators can be described as special symbols that denote a specific operation. The values that the operator works on are referred to as operands.

See this example:

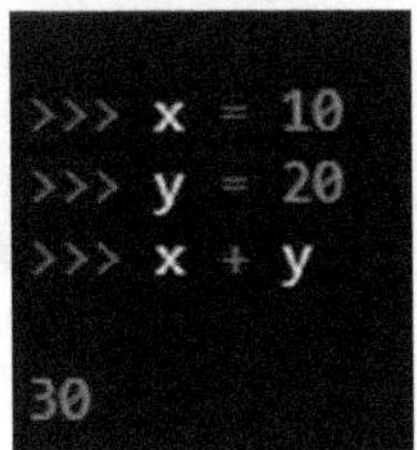

In this example, the + operator computes the sum of x and y. An operand can be a literal value or even a variable which references an object.

When you have a series of operators like x + y – z, this is called an expression. Python allows many operators to combine data objects into expressions. These are shown here:

Arithmetic Operators

Arithmetic operators include +, -, **, //, %, and /.

An example to show some of these operators in a program include:

```
>>> a = 4
>>> b = 3
>>> +a
4
>>> -b
-3
>>> a + b
7
>>> a - b
1
>>> a * b
12
>>> a / b
1.3333333333333333
>>> a % b
1
>>> a ** b
64
```

The output of a standard division (/) is a float, even when the dividend is evenly divisible by the divisor.

If the result of a floor division (//) is positive, it is like the fractional side is truncated off, leaving the integer part. When the result is negative, it has to be rounded down to the next smallest integer:

```
>>> a = 4
>>> b = 3
>>> +a
4
>>> -b
-3
>>> a + b
7
>>> a - b
1
>>> a * b
12
>>> a / b
1.3333333333333333
>>> a % b
1
>>> a ** b
64
```

Comparison Operators

These operators include ==, <=, >,!=, < and >=. Examples of comparison operators include:

```
>>> a = 10
>>> b = 20
>>> a == b
False
>>> a != b
True
>>> a <= b
True
>>> a >= b
False

>>> a = 30
>>> b = 30
>>> a == b
True
>>> a <= b
True
>>> a >= b
True
```

Typically, comparison operators are commonly used in Boolean contexts such as conditional and loop statements to guide program flow.

Equality Comparison-Floating-Point Values

The values of a float object stored internally may not be accurately what you think it can be. As a result, it is a waste of time to compare floating-point values for exact equality. Take, for example:

```
>>> x = 1.1 + 2.2
>>> x == 3.3
False
```

The inner representation of addition operands doesn't reflect exactly to 1.1 and 2.2, and thus you cannot depend on x to make a comparison to 3.3.

The right way to check if two floating-point values are "equal" is to determine if they are close to each other. For example:

```
>>> tolerance = 0.00001
>>> x = 1.1 + 2.2
>>> abs(x - 3.3) < tolerance
True
```

abs () displays an absolute value. If the difference in absolute value between the two numbers is less than a certain tolerance, they are near to be said to be equal.

Logical Operators

The logical operators like or, not, and, "and" change and combine expressions computed in Boolean context to calculate more complex operations.

Logical Expressions including Boolean Operands

There are specific objects and expressions within Python that are of Boolean type. In other words, they are equivalent to one of Python objects False or True. Take, for example:

Explanation of logical expressions that include or, not, and "and" is simple when the operands are Boolean.

See how they work in a program:

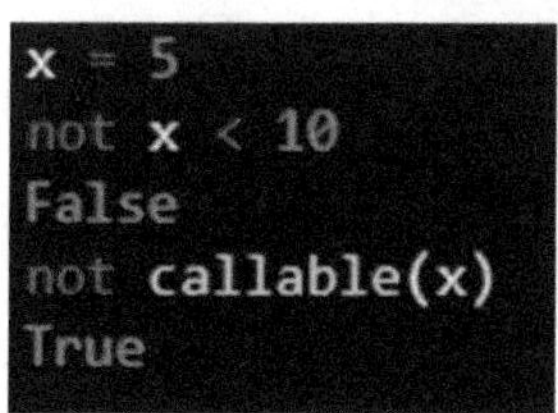

```
x = 5
not x < 10
False
not callable(x)
True
```

Operand	Value	Logical Expression	Value
x < 10	True	not x < 10	False
Callable (x)	False	not callable (x)	True

Computation of Non-Boolean Values in a Boolean Context

Most expressions and objects aren't equal to True or False. Even so, they cannot be determined in a Boolean context to be "falsy" or "truthy."

Well, what is true and what isn't?

In python, this is considered false when computed in Boolean context:

- The Boolean value False.
- An empty string.
- The unique value represented by the Python None keyword.
- Any value that is numerically zero.

Nearly all other objects defined in Python is considered as true.

You can tell the "truthiness" of an expression or object using the built-in bool () function. The bool () returns True if the argument is true, and False when it is Falsy.

The Built-in Composite Data Object

Python has built-in composite data types known as dict, set, tuple, and list. These can be described as "container" type data that host other objects. An object of this type is said to be false; it is empty and true if it is non-empty.

Logical Expressions that Include Non-Boolean Operands

Non-Boolean values can be altered and combined by and, or, and not. The output depends on the "truthiness" of the operands.

"not" **and Non-Boolean Operands**

The following is what happens for non-Boolean value x:

If x is	not x is
"truthy"	False
"falsy"	True

Some more complex examples:

```
>>> x = 3
>>> bool(x)
True
>>> not x
False

>>> x = 0.0
>>> bool(x)
False
>>> not x
True
```

Compound Logical Expressions and Short-Circuit Evaluation

At the moment you have seen expressions that have a single or OR and operator and comprise of two operands:

a or b

a and b

Multiple logical operands and operators can be integrated to develop compound logical expressions.

The Compound "Or" Expressions

Take a look at this expression:

```
x1 or x2 or x3 or … xn
```

This expression is true if one of the xi is true.

In this expression, Python implements a methodology known as short-circuit evaluation. The xi operands are computed in order from left to right. Once it is verified to be true, the whole expression is considered to be true. At this stage, Python stops and no more terms are determined. The value of the whole expression is the xi that completed the evaluation.

Here is an example to describe the short-circuit evaluation. Assume that you have a simple "identity" function f () that does the following:

- F () accepts a single argument
- It outputs the argument to the console
- It returns the argument passed to it as the return value.

For example:

```
>>> f(0)
-> f(0) = 0
0

>>> f(False)
-> f(False) = False
False

>>> f(1.5)
-> f(1.5) = 1.5
1.5
```

Since f () will return the argument passed to it, it can make the expression truthy or falsy by defining the value of arg that is truthy or falsy. Also, f () outputs its argument to the console, which proves whether or not it was called.

Now, take a look at the following compound logical expression:

```
>>> f(0) or f(False) or f(1) or f(2) or f(3)
-> f(0) = 0
-> f(False) = False
-> f(1) = 1
1
```

The Python interpreter will first determine f (0); the result is 0. A numeric value of 0 is false. This expression isn't true yet, and thus, the computation starts from left to right. The next operand, f (False), will return False. This is also false, and the evaluation continues.

Chapter 7: Python Strings

Strings consist of more than one character. A string can be a constant or a variable. A string data type is the main unit of programming.

Create and Print Strings

Strings are surrounded by either ‘or “. For that reason, to define a string, you need to enclose it with single or double quotes.

For example:

“The first program.”

‘Second program.’

It is up to you to decide if you want to use single or double quotes. The only thing you need to ensure is that you become consistent.

String Concatenation

String concatenation is joining strings to create a new string. The + operator is useful when you want to perform string concatenation. Don’t forget that if you use numbers, the + operator becomes an addition operator.

Example of how to concatenate strings:

Print (“Come” + “Back to school”)

Still, you can place whitespace between strings.

When it comes to string concatenation, avoid using the + operator with diverse data types. For example:

Print (“First program” + 34)

This will output an error message.

But if you want to create a string like “feel23”, you can do so by enclosing the number 23 in quotes. This will make it a string instead of an integer. Changing numbers into strings for concatenation is important when working with zip codes.

If you combine more than one string, you get a new string to use in the whole program.

Replication of String

Situations occur that demand the use of Python to automate functions and one way to do this is by repeating a string multiple times. You can accomplish this with the * operator.

The * operator does a different function if used with numbers.

When you use it with a single string and integer, the * becomes the string replication operator. It will repeat a single string different times you want via the integer you offer.

For instance: This code will print the name Python 7 times without typing 7 times:

Print (“Python” * 7)

Using string replication, you can repeat a different string times you want.

How to Store String Variables?

Variables refer to symbols which one can hold data in a program. Think of variables as empty boxes that you enter data or value. As said before, strings are data, and you can use them to take the space of variables. Declaring a string as a variable can simplify the process of using strings in the whole of Python programs.

To keep a string within a variable, you need to allocate a variable to a string. For example:

My_string = "My son likes Pizza."

My_string is a variable. Now you can proceed to print My_string which stores the data in string format.

Print(My_string)

This will output the result: My son likes Pizza.

Using variables in place of strings eliminates the need to retype a string every time you want to use it. This simplifies the process of coding and makes it easy to manipulate strings inside a program.

Uppercase and Lowercase Strings

In the strings functions, there is the function str.upper () and str.lower () which outputs a string with all letters converted either to upper-case or lower-case letters. Since strings are "immutable," these functions create a new string.

Let us change the string "Wake up" to become upper case:

my_string = "wake up"

Print(my_string.upper())

Output

WAKE UP

Next, let us change the string to lower case:

Print(my_string.lower())

Output

wake up

The two string functions: str.upper() and str.lower() functions simplify the process of evaluation and string comparison by making the case consistent. That way, when a user writes their name in small letters, it is still possible to tell whether the name is in the database by looking at all-upper-case names.

Boolean Methods

Python consist of string methods used to determine Boolean value. These methods are important when you want to create forms for users to complete. If we are requesting for a postcode, you will only want to accept a numeric string.

It is important to verify whether characters are upper case, title case, or lower case because it improves the process of sorting data. Additionally, it creates room to standardize data collected by gathering and changing strings.

The Boolean string functions are important when you want to check if something that a user type suits a specific parameter.

Computing the Length Of A String

The len () function will count the number of characters in a string. This method is critical if you want to apply minimum or maximum password lengths. For instance, to truncate larger strings to fit specific limits for application in abbreviations.

To illustrate this method, you will determine the length of a sentence-long string:

```
open_source = "Sammy contributes to open source."
print(len(open_source))

Output
33
```

In this example, the variable open_source is set to equal the string and then the variable is passed to len() method using len(open_source). The method is then passed to print () to determine the output on the screen from the program.

Remember that character enclosed with single or double marks, including whitespace characters and symbols. These will be counted using the len() function.

Other ways you can use to change strings in Python is by using str.split(), str.join(), and str.replace () functions.

The str.join() function joins two strings but in a method in which it passes one string to another.

Whitespace

This is characters which the computer knows but readers cannot see. The most common type of whitespace is newlines, spaces, and tabs.

It is easy to create space because you have been using it since the time you have used computers. Newlines and tabs represent unique character combinations.

You can use tabs anyplace you want in a string.

The character combination for tabs is "\t" while a new line is represented by "\n."

Stripping a White Space

In most instances, you will let users type text into a box, and then read the text and use it. It is simple for people to apply extra whitespace at the start or end of their text. Whitespace comprises of newlines, tabs, and spaces.

In general, it is good to remove this whitespace from strings before you begin to work with them.

Working with Strings

String Literals

Including string values in a Python code is an easy thing. It starts and ends with a single quote. But the question is, how you can apply a quote inside a string? If you type "That is Mark's car." It will not work because Python considers the end of the string as Mark and the remaining section is invalid. Luckily, there are many ways to enter strings.

Double Quotes

Strings can start and end with double quotes, just like it happens with single quotes. However, the advantage of double quotes is that the string can include a single quote character within it. Type the following code into the Python interactive shell:

>>> spam = “That is Mark’s cat.”

Since a string starts with a double quote, Python is aware that the single quote belongs to the string and doesn’t end the string. But if you want to apply both single and double quotes in a string, you will have to apply escape characters.

Escape Characters

An escape character will allow you to include characters that are hard to insert a string. An escape character is made up of a backslash and the character you would like to include to the string. Although it has two characters, it is still called a singular escape character. For instance, the escape character for a single quote is \’. You can include this character into a string that starts and ends with a single quote. To learn how escape characters operate, type this code into the Python shell:

>>> spam = 'Say hello to Bob\'s mother.'

Python can tell from the backlash in a single quote in Bob\’s; this single quote is not the end of the string value. The escape characters \’ and \” allow you to include single quotes and double quotes within your strings.

Raw Strings

You can include r before the start of quotation mark of a string to create a raw string. A raw string will eliminate all escape characters and print backlash that occurs in the string. For example:

>>> print(r'That is Joyce\'s car.')

That is Joyce\'s car.

Since this is a raw string, Python treats the backslash as a member of the string and not at the beginning of an escape character. Raw strings are useful if you type string values that have numerous backslashes like the strings applied for regular expressions.

Multiline Strings

Although you can apply the \n escape character to insert a new line into a string, it is straightforward to apply multiline strings. A multiline string in Python starts and ends with three single quotes, or sometimes three double quotes. Any tabs, quotes or newlines located between the "triple quotes" can be said to members of the string. The rules for Python indentation blocks do not work inside a multiline string.

Type the following in your file editor:

```
print('''Dear Alice,

Eve's cat has been arrested for catnapping, cat burglary, and extortion.

Sincerely,
Bob''')
```

If you run this code, you will get the following result:

```
Dear Alice,


Eve's cat has been arrested for catnapping, cat burglary, and extortion.


Sincerely,
Bob
```

Keep in mind that a single quote character in Eve's doesn't have to be escaped. It is optional to escape single and double quotes in a raw string. A print () call would show identical text, but it doesn't apply a multiline string.

Multiline Comments

Even if the hash character indicates the start of a comment for the remaining line, a multiline string is always used for comments that extend multiple lines. Below is a genuine Python code:

```
"""This is a test Python program.
Written by Al Sweigart al@inventwithpython.com

This program was designed for Python 3, not Python 2.
"""

def spam():
    """This is a multiline comment to help
    explain what the spam() function does."""
    print('Hello!')
```

Stripping Strings And Indexes

Consider a string like 'Hello world!' as a list, and every character inside the string is an item with an equivalent index.

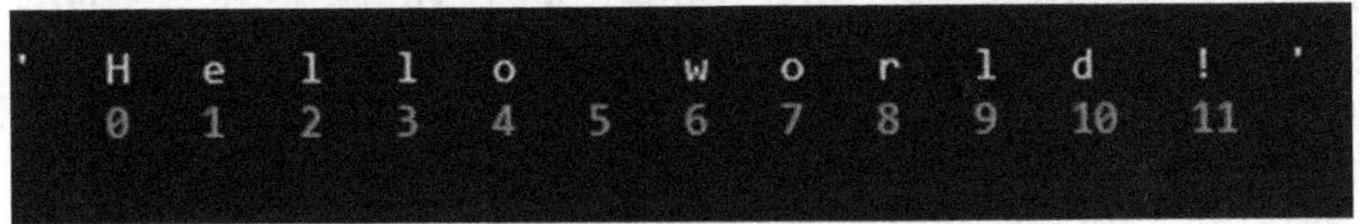

In this example, space and exclamation mark are also counted. This gives you a total of 12.

Enter the following code:

```
>>> spam = 'Hello world!'
>>> spam[0]
'H'
>>> spam[4]
'o'
>>> spam[-1]
'!'
>>> spam[0:5]
'Hello'
>>> spam[:5]
'Hello'
>>> spam[6:]
'world!'
```

Directly addressing an index gives you a character stored in that point. If you apply a range, the starting index must be counted, too.

Something else that you must remember is that slicing a string doesn't change the beginning of the string.

You can retain a slice from a certain variable in a separate variable. Try to enter the following into the interactive shell:

```
>>> spam = 'Hello world!'
>>> fizz = spam[0:5]
>>> fizz
'Hello'
```

Chapter 8: Python Tuples

Tuples are like data sequences with some little difference to lists. Tuples are immutable. In other words, you cannot change, modify, or delete the elements. The syntax that affirms it is a tuple instead of a list is that the elements of a tuple are positioned inside parentheses and not brackets.

The tuple is the default type of sequence in Python. Thus, if I arrange three values here, the computer will consider the new variable as a tuple. Still, we can say the three values will be organized into a tuple. For the same reason, you can allocate various values to the same number of variables.

The same way it can be done for lists, it is possible to index values by specifying their position inside the brackets.

Additionally, you can still include Python tuples inside the lists. Then, every tuple becomes a different element inside the list.

Python tuples resemble lists but there are small differences that you don't need to overlook.

They can be significant when you handle various comma separated values. For example, if you set age and years of school as variables, and you have the correct numbers in a string format, separated by a comma. The split method with the correct indication inside the parentheses will allocate 30 as the value for age and 17 as the number of years in school. We can output the two variables separately to verify the result.

Everything looks correct—great!

Finally, functions can generate tuples in the form of return values. This is important because a function can only display a single tuple having multiple values.

Chapter 9: Conditional Execution

Most of the program examples used so far run the same statements no matter the input entered. The programs tend to use a linear sequence where statement1 executes, followed by statement2 and so forth until the time when the last statement is executed, and the program runs. This chapter will look at program features that allow optional execution of statements.

Boolean Expressions

Also known as a predicate, these expressions may include at least one possible value. The name Boolean originates from George Boole—a British mathematician. If you study discrete mathematics, you will learn more about Boolean algebra, which focuses on logical expressions operations. Boolean expressions are useful for creating interesting programs even though they may appear limited when compared to numeric expressions.

As said before, Boolean expressions in Python language include True and False. In the Python shell, bool is the class that represents Python's Boolean expressions.

You already know that the simplest Boolean expression comprises of False and True. An expression that likens numeric expressions for equality or inequality is still a Boolean expression. The simplest Boolean expressions apply relational operators to compare two expressions. The simplest type of Boolean expression involves relational operators to make a comparison of two expressions.

Expressions such as 5 < 10 are valid but of little significance because 5 is always less than 10. The True expression is simple and less likely to bring confusion among readers. Since it is possible for variables to get new values at the time of program execution, Boolean expressions are relevant when the true values depend on values of one or more variables.

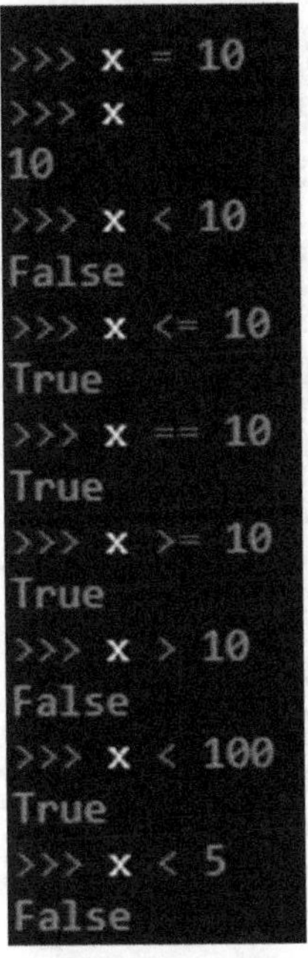

>>> x = 10
>>> x
10
>>> x < 10
False
>>> x <= 10
True
>>> x == 10
True
>>> x >= 10
True
>>> x > 10
False
>>> x < 100
True
>>> x < 5
False

The first input assigns the variable x to 10. The other expressions test out the relational operators.

The If Statement

Sometimes, you may think that the Boolean expressions previously discussed are of little use in practical scenarios. However, Booleans are significant for a program to adjust its behavior at the time of execution. In most practical and useful programs, it is hard for Boolean expressions to miss.

Execution errors in programming emerge because of logic errors. One way in which these errors arise is when you input zero for the divisor. Luckily, programmers can make important steps to make sure that the division by zero does not happen.

```
print('Please enter two numbers to divide.')
dividend = int(input('Please enter the first number to divide: '))
divisor = int(input('Please enter the second number to divide: '))
# If possible, divide them and report the result
if divisor != 0:
print(dividend, '/', divisor, "=", dividend/divisor)
```

In the above program, the program may fail to execute the print statement depending on the input which the user enters. For example: If a user enters zero as the input for the second number. It will print nothing after the value is entered:

```
Please enter two numbers to divide.
Please enter the first number to divide: 32
Please enter the second number to divide: 0
```

The last line of code in this program starts with the if statement. In other words, it is not a must for this statement to execute the code inside it. In the following case, the if statement will only evaluate the print statement when the value of the variable divisor is a non-zero.

This leads to the Boolean expression: divisor!= 0

This expression decides whether the program will evaluate the statement inside the if block. In case the divisor is a non-zero, the program displays the message. If not, the program will output nothing after the input.

The standard format for if the statement is as follows:

```
If (condition):

 Block
```

"If" is a python keyword that indicates the start of the statement.

The condition has the expression that will determine if the body is executed. It is important to include a colon immediately after the condition.

The block includes statements to be executed. It is necessary to indent statements inside the block.

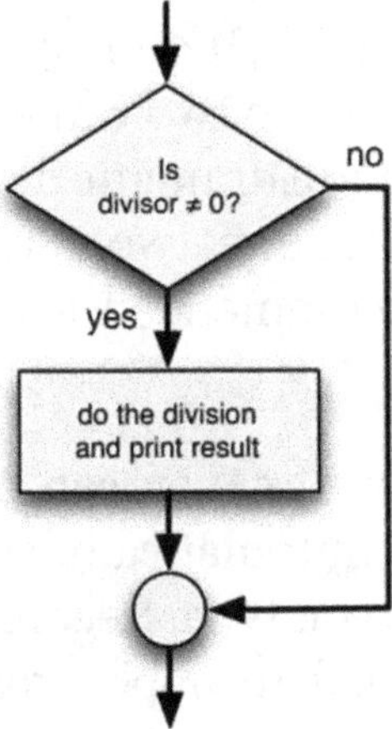

Also, the if has to be indented with enough spaces than the line that starts the if statement. Technically, the block belongs to the if statement. Sometimes, it is referred to as the body of the if statement.

The rules of Python demand that the block should be indented. In case the block has only one statement, some Python developers include it on the same line with the if. For example:

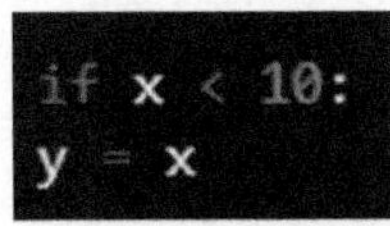

```
if x < 10:
y = x
```

This can be rewritten as:

```
if x < 10: y = x
```

But it cannot be written as:

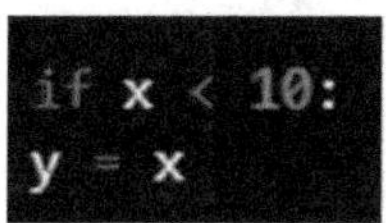

```
if x < 10:
y = x
```

Because the absence of indentation hides the optional execution of the assignment statement. Indentation describes the way Python decides the statement that should be part of the block.

What is the count of spaces to indent? Python rules require at least one but other Python developers use two while four is the most popular. However, those who like a dramatic display apply eight. If you are lost on whether to use one, two, four, or eight, then we advise you to apply the recommended four space by Python style.

In most of the programming text editors, you can navigate to the Tab key and insert the spaces automatically so that you don't have to count the spaces while you type. Regardless of the indent distance, you select, you need to apply this distance consistently in the entire Python program.

Make sure that you don't combine spaces and tabs while indenting statements inside a block. Python 3 forbids the mixing of tabs and spaces while indenting. Also, be aware that in most editors, it is hard to tell between a tab and a series of spaces. The number of spaces that is equivalent to the spacing of a tab is different between editors. In general, a tab stop indicates a fixed distance running from the left side of the editing window. Most editors come with multiple tab stops. For example, the first tab stop can be eight characters from the beginning of the line, followed by a sequence of tab stops, each staying at a distance of eight characters from the previous tab stop.

Additionally, most editors only let the user change the settings of the location of the tab stops. Pressing the tab key in the editor may make the cursor inside the editing window to move to the next tab stop inside the line. On the other side, the space bar will always shift the cursor one character to the right.

Well, you may be wondering why indentation that combines tabs and spaces is a big issue that is not allowed in Python? Try and create a Python file in one editor and open the same in a different editor that has tab stops reconfigured differently. Lines perfectly indented in the initial editor would be disarranged in the new editor. Rather than code indented using four spaces inside one editor, it would accurately appear the same in the other editor.

Python version 3 supports the application of tabs for indentation. But you cannot combine them with spaces inside the same source file. In most editors, there is a setting to automatically replace a certain number of spaces when a user touches on the Tab key.

As a bonus to Python developers, the concept of true and false in Python goes beyond what we take as Boolean expressions. For example:

```
if 1:
print('one')
```

This statement will print one. But the statement:

```
if 0:
print('zero')
```

Will not print anything. The reason is that the integer value zero is considered to be false by Python. Also, the floating point 0.0 is considered false but other floating point values are considered to be true. An empty string such as '' or "is also false, and a non-empty string is considered as true. Python expression can act as a condition for an if statement.

The If.... Else Statement

Sometimes, you may want to generate great feedback to the user to show why something is false or any other explanation. This is the point where the ***if*** statement becomes useful. It has an optional else block that is only active when the ***if*** condition is false.

Consider the following example:

```
# Get two integers from the user
dividend = int(input('Please enter the number to divide: '))
divisor = int(input('Please enter dividend: '))
# If possible, divide them and report the result
if divisor != 0:
print(dividend, '/', divisor, "=", dividend/divisor)
else:
print('Division by zero is not allowed')
```

In this program, the else block contains an alternate code that the program implements when the condition is false.

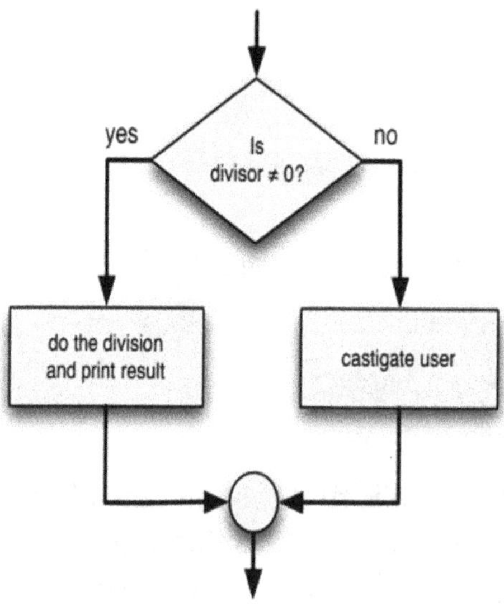

The last else block in the example highlighted notifies the user that a division by zero is not allowed. A different application can deal with the problem using a new approach like replace a default value for the divisor rather than the zero.

The format of the if...else statement is:

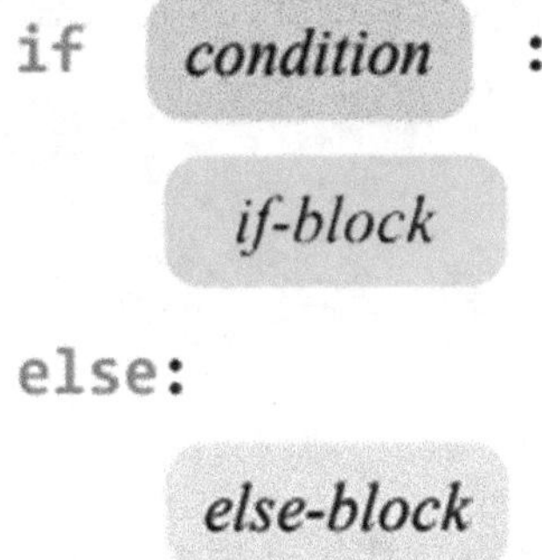

The Pass Statement

In some instances, new programmers try to use the if...else statement when they can use the simple if statement. For example:

In this code snippet, the programmer wishes to do nothing if the value of the variable x is less than zero. But in case the value is more than zero, the program would like to print the value of x.

```
if x < 0:
# Do nothing (This will not work!)
else:
print(x)
```

In this particular program, if the value of the variable x is less than zero, the code should print nothing. But this particular program isn't correct. The if...else statement has an else block but it doesn't have an if block. The comment section isn't part of the Python statement.

Python has a unique statement called pass. The meaning of this statement is to do nothing. You can include the pass statement inside your code, in particular where you want a statement but don't want the program to execute anything. So this code snippet can be made legal using a pass statement as follows:

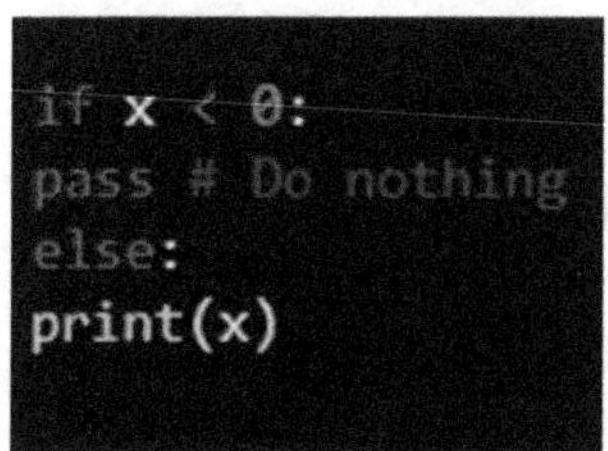
if x < 0:
pass # Do nothing
else:
print(x)

Although the pass statement validates the code, you can optimize its logic by applying a simple if statement. Mathematically, when the expression x < y is false, then it should be x >= y. By inverting the truth value of the relation inside the condition, this code can be well defined as:

```
if x >= 0:

print(x)
```

Therefore, anytime you want to create an if...else statement using an empty if body, then you need to do the following:

1. Reverse the truth value of the condition.
2. Let the proposed else body become the if body.
3. Remove the else

In cases where you may want to apply a non-functional else block, don't change the condition but remove the else and else block.

In Python, the pass statement is important to keep the place for the code to appear in the future. For example:

```
if x < 0:
pass # TODO: print an appropriate warning message to be determined
else:
print(x)
```

In the following code snippet, the programmer wishes to create an if block, but the right type of code in the if block is yet to be defined. As a result, the pass statement acts a placeholder for the upcoming code. The comments in this code describe more about the program.

Floating Point in Equality Operators

The task of the equality operator is to check for precise accuracy. This is a big problem when dealing with floating-point numbers because they aren't accurate.

```
d1 = 1.11 - 1.10
d2 = 2.11 - 2.10
print('d1 =', d1, ' d2 =', d2)
if d1 == d2:
print('Same')
else:
print('Different')
```

If you apply the knowledge of mathematics, the following equality should stand:

```
1.11-1.10 = 0.01 = 2.11-2.10
```

The result of the first print statement revives the perception of floating point numbers:

```
d1 = 0.010000000000000009 d2 = 0.009999999999999787
```

In this example, the expression d1==d2 determines the accuracy of the equality operator, and hence, it will indicate that the two expressions are different.

The best way to use to confirm whether floating-point numbers are equivalent is to look at the absolute value of the two numbers.

Nested Conditionals

The statements inside the if, or else block can be any Python statement. We can apply the nested if statement to create arbitrarily advanced program logic. Take, for instance, the following program that checks whether a number is in the range between 0-10:

```
value = int(input("Please enter an integer value in the range 0...10: ")
if value >= 0: # First check
if value <= 10: # Second check
print("In range")
print("Done")
```

In this program:

- The running program first evaluates the condition. Let us say that the first value is found to be lower than zero, it will not move to the second condition, but it will shift to the next statement in the outer if.
- If the program determines that the value of the variable is greater or equivalent to the variable, it will print the statement inside the if block.

We conclude that the second if it is enclosed within the first if. The first if is external if and the second if is considered the inner if. Keep in mind that the full if the statement has been indented one level from the outer if statement. In other words, the if's block plus the ("In range") statement has been indented two levels down the outer if statement.

Don't forget that four space indentation style requires that you have fours space distance for each indentation inside the program.

Both conditions that belong to the if block must be fulfilled in the In range message that should be printed. From this angle, it is possible to rewrite the program using a single if statement. For example:

```
value = int(input("Please enter an integer value in the range 0...10: ")
if value >= 0 and value <= 10: # Only one, slightly more complicated check
print("In range")
print("Done")
```

This program relies on the and operator to validate both conditions simultaneously. The logic for this statement is simple when you use one if statement instead of an advanced Boolean expression in the condition.

The if condition in this program can be expressed in a compact manner as 0 <= value <= 10.

Sometimes, it is hard to determine the logic of a program. For example, it is impossible to rewrite the previous example using a single if statement.

```
value = int(input("Please enter an integer value in the range 0...10: ")
if value >= 0: # First check
if value <= 10: # Second check
print(value, "is in range")
else:
print(value, "is too large")
else:
print(value, "is too small")
print("Done")
```

This program describes a specific message rather than a simple message of acceptance. Out of the three messages, at least one is displayed depending on what value is in the variable.

Computers interpret data in binary style. This style is straightforward compared to the decimal number system. While the binary system used two digits, the decimal system requires digits from 0-9. Even when there are no digits, no decimal integer will lack binary representation.

With the presence of 10 digits to execute, the decimal number system can tell the difference between place values and powers of 10.

Multi-Decision Statements

The simple if...else statement can choose between implementing two paths. This program is great to demonstrate how to choose from three options. Suppose one of the many actions should be executed?

Then you will need to have nested if...else statements and the way nested if is used shown here:

```
value = int(input("Please enter an integer in the range 0...5: "))
if value < 0:
print("Too small")
else:
if value == 0:
print("zero")
else:
if value == 1:
print("one")
else:
if value == 2:
print("two")
else:
if value == 3:
print("three")
else:
if value == 4:
print("four")
else:
if value == 5:
print("five")
else:
print("Too large")
print("Done")
```

Notice the following from this program:

- The program will display one of the eight messages based on what the user enters as input.
- Each if block is made up of a single printing statement, and an else block. Only the last if that doesn't have an if statement. The control logic dictates the program execution to determine every condition in turn. The first condition that is met has its corresponding if body executed. If no conditions fulfill the input, the program will resort to displaying the "Too large message."

From this program, a huge code shifts to the right as more conditions are checked. Fortunately, Python has a multi-way conditional construct known as the if/elif/else that will allow a manageable textual structure for programs that determine a lot of conditions.

```
value = int(input("Please enter an integer in the range 0...5: "))
if value < 0:
print("Too small")
elif value == 0:
print("zero")
elif value == 1:
print("one")
elif value == 2:
print("two")
elif value == 3:
print("three")
elif value == 4:
print("four")
elif value == 5:
print("five")
else:
print("Too large")
print("Done")
```

The term *elif* is extracted from else and if. If you can pronounce *elif* as else if, then you will be able to see how you can change the code snippet.

The multi-way if/elif/else statement is helpful when you want to choose a single block of code from various options. The if a section of an if/elif/else statement is vital. The else part is optional.

The general format for the if/elif/else statement is:

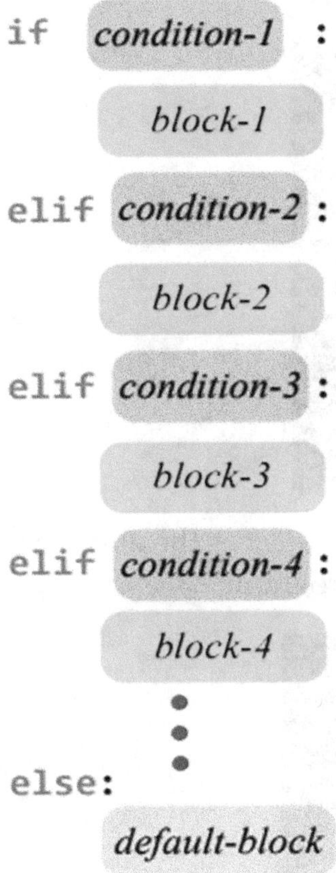
if
condition-1
:
block-1
elif
condition-2
:
block-2
elif
condition-3
:
block-3
elif
condition-4
:
block-4
else:
default-block

Point to note: An if/elif/else statement that contains an optional else will implement exactly one of its block. The first condition that computes to true decides which block to run. An if/elif/else statement that removes the else block may stop to check the code in any of its blocks in case none of the condition evaluates to True.

Sometimes new programmers will confuse multi-way if/elif/else with a series of simple statements. This program will print nothing if the user enters an integer out of range but it will print the matching English word.

```
# Use a mult-way conditional statement
value = int(input())
if value == 0:
print("zero")
elif value == 1:
print("one")
elif value == 2:
print("two")
elif value == 3:
print("three")
elif value == 4:
print("four")
elif value == 5:
print("five")
print("Done")
```

Now take a look at this program. It replaces the elifs with ifs. It behaves exactly like the previous program:

```
# Use sequential conditional statements
value = int(input())
if value == 0:
print("zero")
if value == 1:
print("one")
if value == 2:
print("two")
if value == 3:
print("three")
if value == 4:
print("four")
if value == 5:
print("five")
print("Done")
```

Although these two programs do the same thing, the previous program is much better. Why?

The first program only performs two comparisons before making a decision and printing the message Done. On the other hand, the second program must verify each conditional expression inside the program before printing the same message. While it is hard to notice the difference, in a large complex program, the additional computation may highly affect the run time of the application. The main thing is the picture it creates to new programmers that the sequential ifs is equivalent to the multi-way if/elifs.

To remove this notion, compare the following programs:

```
num = int(input("Enter a number: "))
if num == 1:
print("You entered one")
elif num == 2:
print("You entered two")
elif num > 5:
print("You entered a number greater than five")
elif num == 7:
print("You entered seven")
else:
print("You entered some other number")
```

In this particular program, when a user inputs 7, the program displays the message "You entered a number greater than five."

In the second program, it converts all the elif to become ifs. This means that when a user inputs 7, the program will display the same message as in the previous example. The only difference is that this program will print an extra message that says, "You entered seven."

```
num = int(input("Enter a number: "))
if num == 1:
print("You entered one")
if num == 2:
print("You entered two")
if num > 5:
print("You entered a number greater than five")
if num == 7:
print("You entered seven")
else:
print("You entered some other number")
```

From the following programs, you can see that the multi-way conditional statements act differently from the sequential ifs.

Conditional Expressions

Let us look at the following code:

```
if a != b:
c = d
else:
c = e
```

This code will store one of the two potential values in c. Python has an alternative to the if/else known as the conditional expression. A conditional expression will compute one of two values based on the Boolean condition. This code can be rewritten as:

```
c = d if a != b else e
```

The general syntax of this conditional expression is:

```
expression-1 if condition else expression-2
```

- The expression-1 holds the entire value of the expression if it is true.
- The condition is a normal Boolean expression that may appear inside an if statement.
- Expression-2 is the entire value of the expression in case the result is false.

Some people say that conditional expressions aren't easy to read like a normal if/else statement. No matter what, most Python programmers don't use it often because it is specific. The standard if/else block can feature numerous statements, but the items in the conditional expression are restricted to a single straightforward expression.

Errors Found In Conditional Statements

Examine the following compound conditional carefully:

```
value > 0 and value <= 10
```

One of the most common mistakes that programmers make is confusing the logical **and** and the logical **or.**

Take a look at this:

```
x > 0 or x <= 10
```

Which values do you think can make this expression true and also make it false? The fact is that this expression will be true regardless of what the x value is. This is an example of a tautology.

Now, assume x is a number, can you think of a number that can make the expression false? At least one of the subexpression will be true.

Another common error committed by Python programmers is called contradictions. Assume you don't want to include values in a given range. For example, you don't want values in the range 0-10. Can this Boolean expression complete the task?

```
# All but 0, 1, 2, ..., 10
if value < 0 and value > 10:
print(value)
```

If you carefully examine the condition, you will learn that it cannot be true. Is there a number that can be less than zero and greater than 10 simultaneously? Of course, none. In this case, this expression can be said to be a contradiction and a complex way of illustrating False. To fix this code snippet, you need to substitute the **and** operator with **or** operator.

When it comes to operator precedence, the logical or, not and have a lower precedence than the comparison operators. What if you want to display the word OK when the variable x is 1, 2, or 3:

```
if x == 1 or 2 or 3:
print("OK")
```

But the value of x is irrelevant. The code snippet will always print OK no matter what the value of x is. Because the == operator has the highest precedence than the or, Python will consider this expression as:

```
x == 1 or 2 or 3
```

This expression x == 1 can both be true or false. However, the integer 2 is considered true. Any true value included in a series of subexpressions joined by or will make the entire expression true.

The right way to illustrate the initial statement is as follows:

```
if x == 1 or x == 2 or x == 3:
print("OK")
```

Although the Boolean expression looks verbose, that is the right way of writing Python. Keep in mind that every subexpression includes a Boolean expression but not an integer value.

In many programs, you may find programmers making small spelling error mistakes. This generally makes a program to fail to run.

The keys M and N on the English keyboard are very close to each other. Therefore, it is one of the most common typographical errors that programmers make. They press N when they wanted to press M.

As the length of our programs increases, it can be very difficult to track down a misspelled word that causes an error in a program. Fortunately, there are tools that have been developed to help programmers deal with this kind of challenges. Some of these Python tools include Pylint.

The Advanced Nature of Logic

Python language comes with tools to help build complex conditional statements. It is crucial to avoid the desire to make things more complex. When you create Boolean expressions using "or", "not", and "and", it makes you create somewhat complex conditions. There are many different methods to attain the same effect. For example, all these Boolean expressions are equal.

```
not (a == b and c != d)
not (a == b and not (c == d))
not (a == b) or not (c != d)
a != b or c == d
```

Although these expressions express the same thing, they have a different level of complexity.

Some instances demand a complex logic to attain the correct behavior of a program. However, the easiest logic that works is favorable than one, which is complex because:

- It is easy to understand simple logic.
- It is easy to write and make simple logic work because you can understand it. However, longer expressions that are a bit advanced increase the risk of making spelling errors that show up as logic errors. These are one of the most difficult errors to track down.
- Not forgetting, a simple logic improves efficiency. Every Boolean expression and relational comparison demands a repetition in the machine. So, if you use simple logic, the entire process will be fast and efficient. For example:

```
not (a == b and not (c == d))
```

This expression computes five different operations. In case a fails to equal b, it will only execute two operations because of something called short-circuit Boolean operation of the and. Now draw a comparison between this expression and the previous one:

```
a != b or c == d
```

A running program can compute this expression faster because it consists of three computations, that being the highest. However, if a fails to equal b, the computation will short-circuit the or, and determine only the != operation.

Another reason why you need to go for simpler logic is that it is easy to change it.

Chapter 10: Iteration

The term iteration in programming refers to the repetition of lines of code. It is a useful concept in programming that helps determine solutions to problems. Iteration and conditional execution is the reference for algorithm development.

While Statement

The following program counts to five, and prints a number on every output line.

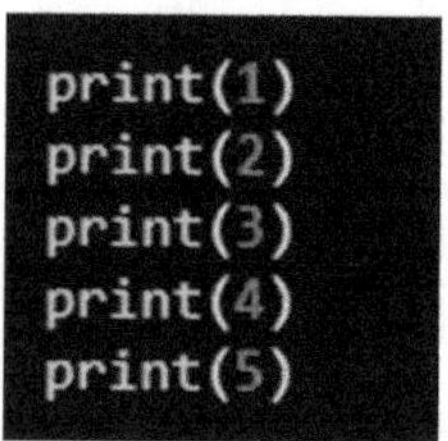

```
print(1)
print(2)
print(3)
print(4)
print(5)
```

Well, how can you write a code that can count to 10,000? Are you going to copy paste and change the 10, 000 printing statements? You can but that is going to be tiresome. But counting is a common thing and computers count large values. So there must be an efficient way to do so. What you need to do is to print the value of a variable and start to increment the variable, and repeat the process until you get 10,000. This process of implementing the same code, again and again, is known as looping. In Python, there is two unique statements, while and for, that support iteration.

Here is a program that uses while statement to count to five:

```
count = 1 # Initialize counter
while count <= 5: # Should we continue?
print(count) # Display counter, then
count += 1 # Increment counter
```

The while statement used in this particular program will repeatedly output the variable count. The program then implements this block of statement five times:

```
print(count)
count += 1
```

After every display of the count variable, the program increases it by one. Finally, after five repetitions, the condition will not be true, and the block of code is not executed anymore.

This line `while count <= 5:` is the opening of the while statement. The expression that follows the while keyword is the condition that determines whether the block is executed. As long as the result of the condition is true, the program will continue to run the code block over and over. But when the condition becomes false, the loop terminates. Also, if the condition is evaluated as false at the start, the program cannot implement the code block inside the body of the loop.

The general syntax of the while statement is:

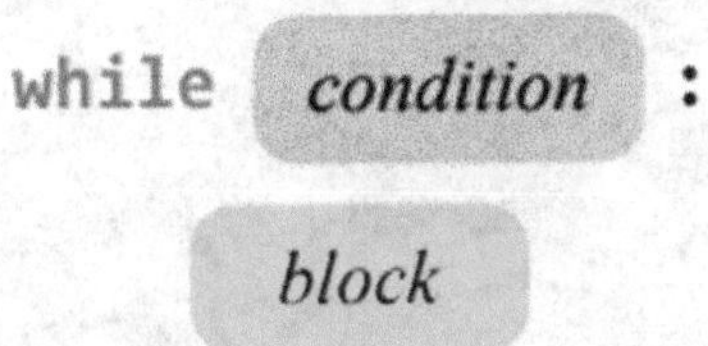

The word while is a Python reserved word that starts the statement.

The condition shows whether the body will be executed or not. A colon (:) has to come after the condition.

A block is made up of one or more statements that should be implemented if the condition is found to be true. All statements that make up the block must be indented one level deeper than the first line of the while statement. Technically, the block belongs to the while statement.

The while statement can resemble the if statements and thus new programmers may confuse the two. Sometimes, they may type if when they wanted to use while. Often, the uniqueness of the two statements shows the problem instantly. But in some nested and advanced logic, this error can be hard to notice.

The running program evaluates the condition before running the while block and then confirms the condition after running the while block. If the condition remains true, the program will continuously run the code in the while block. If initially, the condition is true, the program will run the block iteratively until when the condition is false. This is the point when the loop exits from execution. Below is a program that will count from zero as long as the user wants it to do.

```
# Counts up from zero. The user continues the count by entering
# 'Y'. The user discontinues the count by entering 'N'.
count = 0 # The current count
entry = 'Y' # Count to begin with
while entry != 'N' and entry != 'n':
# Print the current value of count
print(count)
entry = input('Please enter "Y" to continue or "N" to quit: ')
if entry == 'Y' or entry == 'y':
count += 1 # Keep counting
# Check for "bad" entry
elif entry != 'N' and entry != 'n':
print('"' + entry + '" is not a valid choice')
# else must be 'N' or 'n'
```

Here is another program that will let the user type different non-negative integers. If the user types a negative value, the program stops to accept inputs and outputs the total of all nonnegative values. In case a negative number is the first entry, the sum will be zero.

```
# Allow the user to enter a sequence of nonnegative
# integers. The user ends the list with a negative
# integer. At the end the sum of the nonnegative
# numbers entered is displayed. The program prints
# zero if the user provides no nonnegative numbers.
entry = 0 # Ensure the loop is entered
sum = 0 # Initialize sum
# Request input from the user
print("Enter numbers to sum, negative number ends list:")
while entry >= 0: # A negative number exits the loop
entry = int(input()) # Get the value
if entry >= 0: # Is number nonnegative?
sum += entry # Only add it if it is nonnegative
print("Sum =", sum) # Display the sum
```

Let us explore the details of this program:

First, the program uses two variables, sum and entry.

- Entry

At the start, you will initialize the entry to zero because we want the condition entry >=0 of the while statement to be true. Failure to initialize the variable entry, the program will generate a run-time error when it tries to compare entry to zero in the while condition. The variable entry stores the number typed by the user. The value of the variable entry changes every time inside the loop.

- Sum

This variable is one that stores the total of each number entered by the user. For this particular variable, it is initialized to zero in the start because a value of zero shows that it has not evaluated anything. If you don't initialize the variable sum, the program will also generate a run-time error when it tries to apply the +- operator to change the variable. Inside the loop, you can constantly add the user's input values to sum. When the loop completes, the variable sum will feature the total of all nonnegative values typed by the user.

The initialization of the entry to zero plus the condition entry >= 0 of the while ensures that the program will run the body of the while loop only once. The if statement confirms that the program won't add a negative entry to the sum.

When a user types a negative value, the running program may not update the sum variable and the condition of the while will not be true. The loop exits and the program implements the print statement.

This program doesn't store the number of values typed. But it adds the values entered in the variable sum.

```
print("Help! My computer doesn't work!")
done = False # Not done initially
while not done:
print("Does the computer make any sounds (fans, etc.) ")
choice = input("or show any lights? (y/n):")
# The troubleshooting control logic
if choice == 'n': # The computer does not have power
choice = input("Is it plugged in? (y/n):")
if choice == 'n': # It is not plugged in, plug it in
print("Plug it in.")
else: # It is plugged in
choice = input("Is the switch in the \"on\" position? (y/n):")
if choice == 'n': # The switch is off, turn it on!
print("Turn it on.")
else: # The switch is on
choice = input("Does the computer have a fuse? (y/n):")
if choice == 'n': # No fuse
choice = input("Is the outlet OK? (y/n):")
if choice == 'n': # Fix outlet
print("Check the outlet's circuit ")
print("breaker or fuse. Move to a")
print("new outlet, if necessary. ")
else: # Beats me!
print("Please consult a service technician.")
done = True # Nothing else I can do
else: # Check fuse
print("Check the fuse. Replace if ")
print("necessary.")
else: # The computer has power
print("Please consult a service technician.")
done = True # Nothing else I can do
```

A while block occupies a huge percent of this program. The program has a Boolean variable done that regulates the loop. The loop will continue to run as long as done is false. The name of this Boolean variable called a flag. Now, when the flag is raised, the value is true, if not, the value is false.

Don't forget the *not done* is the opposite of the variable *done*.

Definite and Indefinite Loops

Let us look at the following code:

```
n = 1
while n <= 10:
print(n)
n += 1
```

We examine this code and establish the correct number of iterations inside the loop. This type of loop is referred to as a definite loop because we can accurately tell the number of time the loop repeats.

Now, take a look at the following code:

```
n = 1
stop = int(input())
while n <= stop:
print(n)
n += 1
```

In this code, it is hard to establish the number of times it will loop. The number of repetitions relies on the input entered by the user. But it is possible to know the number of repetitions the while loop will make at the point of execution after entering users input before the next execution begins.

For that reason, the loop is said to be a definite loop.

Now compare the previous programs with this one:

```
done = False # Enter the loop at least once
while not done:
entry = int(input()) # Get value from user
if entry == 999: # Did user provide the magic number?
done = True # If so, get out
else:
print(entry) # If not, print it and continue
```

For this program, you cannot tell at any point inside the loop's execution the number of times the iterations can run. The value 999 is known before and after the loop but the value of the entry can be anything the user inputs. The user can decide to input 0 or even 999 and end it. The while statement in this program is a great example of an indefinite loop.

So the while statement is perfect for indefinite loops. While these examples have applied the while statements to demonstrate definite loops, Python has a better option for definite loops. That is none other than the for statement.

The For Statement

The while loop is perfect for indefinite loops. This has been demonstrated in the previous programs, where it is impossible to tell the number of times the while loop will run. Previously, the while loop was used to run a definite loop such as:

```
n = 1
while n <= 10:
print(n)
n += 1
```

In the following code snippet, the print statement will only run 10 times. This code demands three important parts to control the loop:

- Initialization

- Check
- Update

Python language has an efficient method to demonstrate a definite loop. The *for* statement repeats over a series of values. One method to demonstrate a series is to use a tuple. For example:

```
for n in 1, 2, 3, 4, 5, 6, 7, 8, 9, 10:
print(n)
```

This code works the same way as the while loop is shown earlier. In this example, the print statement runs 10 times. The code will print first 1, then 2, and so forth. The last value it prints is 10.

It is always tedious to display all elements of a tuple. Imagine going over all the integers from 1 to 1, 000, and outputting all the elements of the tuple in writing. That would be impractical. Fortunately, Python has an efficient means of displaying a series of integers that assume a consistent pattern.

This code applies the range expression to output integers between 1-10.

```
for n in range(1, 11):
print(n)
```

The range expression (1,11) develops a range object that will let the for loop to allocate the variable n the values 1, 2, ...10.

The line of code in this code snippet is interpreted as "for every integer n in the range $1 \leq n < 11$." In the first execution of the loop, the value of n is 1 inside the block. In the next iteration of the loop, the value of n is 2. The value of n increases by one for each loop. The code inside the block will apply the value of n until it hits 10. The general format for the range expression goes as follows:

range(*begin*, *end*, *step*)

From the general syntax:

- Begin represents the leading value in the range; when it is deleted, the default value becomes 0.
- The end value is one value after the last value. This value is necessary, and should not be deleted.
- Step represents the interval of increase or decrease. The default value for step is 1 if it is deleted.

All the values for begin, step, and end must be integer expressions. Floating-point expressions and other types aren't allowed. The arguments that feature inside the range expression can be literal numbers such as 10, or even variables like m, n, and some complex integer expressions.

One thing good about the range expression is the flexibility it brings. For example:

```
for n in range(21, 0, -3):
print(n, end=' ')

output

21 18 15 12 9 6 3
```

This means that you can use the range to display a variety of sequences.

For range expressions that have a single argument like range(y), the y is the end of the range, while 0 is the beginning value, and then 1 the step value.

For expressions carrying two arguments like range (m, n), m is the begin value, while y is the end of the range. The step value becomes 1.

For expressions that have three arguments like range (m, n, y), m is the begin value, n is the end, and y is the step value.

When it comes to a for loop, the range object has full control on selecting the loop variable each time via the loop.

If you keep a close eye on older Python resources or even online Python example, you are likely to come across the xrange expression. Python version 2 has both the range and xrange. However, Python 3 doesn't have the xrange. In fact, the range expression of Python 3 is like the xrange expression in Python 2.

In Python 2, the range expression builds a data structure known as a list and this process can demand some time for a running program. In Python 2, the xrange expression eliminates the additional time. Hence, it is perfect for a big sequence. When creating loops using the for statement, developers of Python 2 prefer the xrange instead of the range to optimize the functionality of the code.

Still, Python 3 allows permits you to use range without affecting the run-time performance.

We recommend one to use the for loop because it has great potential to loop over integer series because it is a helpful and important role in software development.

Also, the for loop can loop over any iterable object.

Nested Loops

Both for and while loops can include other loops within it. Therefore, it is possible for a loop to be nested inside another loop. To understand how a nested loop operates, take a look at the program that outputs the results of a multiplication table. Students of elementary level depend on times table to master the products of integers that extend to 10 or 12.

In this section, we shall write a multiplication program. This program will be flexible and let the user enter the values that determine the size of the table.

Initially, only the contents of the table shall be printed. But you will have to write a nested loop to help you display the results of the table. While that can seem tough to try out, in this first trial, the program will print only the table rows. Once it prints the rows, then we can continue to add extra features. See the program:

```
# Get the number of rows and columns in the table
size = int(input("Please enter the table size: "))
# Print a size x size multiplication table
for row in range(1, size + 1):
print("Row #", row)
```

Output

```
Please enter the table size: 10
Row #1
Row #2
Row #3
Row #4
Row #5
Row #6
Row #7
Row #8
Row #9
Row #10
```

From the output, you can tell that it is a bit underwhelming.

This program print rows the way we wanted—no extra details for each row.

Now, the next thing we are going to do is to add more features to the program. We want each row to have the numbers.

Here is a refined code:

```
# Get the number of rows and columns in the table
size = int(input("Please enter the table size: "))
# Print a size x size multiplication table
for row in range(1, size + 1):
for column in range(1, size + 1):
product = row*column # Compute product
print(product, end=' ') # Display product
print() # Move cursor to next row
```

A loop is created to display the contents of every row. The external loop controls the total number of rows the program displays.

The output of the refined program:

```
Please enter the table size: 10
1 2 3 4 5 6 7 8 9 10
2 4 6 8 10 12 14 16 18 20
3 6 9 12 15 18 21 24 27 30
4 8 12 16 20 24 28 32 36 40
5 10 15 20 25 30 35 40 45 50
6 12 18 24 30 36 42 48 54 60
7 14 21 28 35 42 49 56 63 70
8 16 24 32 40 48 56 64 72 80
9 18 27 36 45 54 63 72 81 90
10 20 30 40 50 60 70 80 90 100
```

The numbers inside each column aren't organized well but the numbers are in the right positions relative to each other. So we can apply a string formatter to the right justify the numbers. Here is the new code:

```
# Get the number of rows and columns in the table
size = int(input("Please enter the table size: "))
# Print a size x size multiplication table
for row in range(1, size + 1):
for column in range(1, size + 1):
product = row*column # Compute product
print('{0:4}'.format(product), end='') # Display product
print()
```

This code makes the output to look attractive:

```
Please enter the table size: 10
   1   2   3   4   5   6   7   8   9  10
   2   4   6   8  10  12  14  16  18  20
   3   6   9  12  15  18  21  24  27  30
   4   8  12  16  20  24  28  32  36  40
   5  10  15  20  25  30  35  40  45  50
   6  12  18  24  30  36  42  48  54  60
   7  14  21  28  35  42  49  56  63  70
   8  16  24  32  40  48  56  64  72  80
   9  18  27  36  45  54  63  72  81  90
  10  20  30  40  50  60  70  80  90 100
```

Notice the presentation of the table changes based on what the user enters as input.

```
Please enter the table size: 5
   1   2   3   4   5
   2   4   6   8  10
   3   6   9  12  15
   4   8  12  16  20
   5  10  15  20  25
```

Next, let us finalize this program by including a row and column titles as well as lines that enclose the edges of the table. This code adds the relevant changes:

```
# Get the number of rows and columns in the table
size = int(input("Please enter the table size: "))
# Print a size x size multiplication table
# First, print heading: 1 2 3 4 5 etc.
print(" ", end='')
# Print column heading
for column in range(1, size + 1):
print('{0:4}'.format(column), end='') # Display column number
print() # Go down to the next line
# Print line separator: +------------------
print(" +", end='')
for column in range(1, size + 1):
print('----', end='') # Display line
print() # Drop down to next line
# Print table contents
for row in range(1, size + 1):
print('{0:3} |'.format(row), end='') # Print heading for this row
for column in range(1, size + 1):
product = row*column # Compute product
print('{0:4}'.format(product), end='') # Display product
print() # Move cursor to next row
```

The formatted output:

```
Please enter the table size: 10
       1   2   3   4   5   6   7   8   9  10
    +----------------------------------------
  1 |   1   2   3   4   5   6   7   8   9  10
  2 |   2   4   6   8  10  12  14  16  18  20
  3 |   3   6   9  12  15  18  21  24  27  30
  4 |   4   8  12  16  20  24  28  32  36  40
  5 |   5  10  15  20  25  30  35  40  45  50
  6 |   6  12  18  24  30  36  42  48  54  60
  7 |   7  14  21  28  35  42  49  56  63  70
  8 |   8  16  24  32  40  48  56  64  72  80
  9 |   9  18  27  36  45  54  63  72  81  90
 10 |  10  20  30  40  50  60  70  80  90 100
```

If a user enters 7:

```
Please enter the table size: 7
       1   2   3   4   5   6   7
   +----------------------------
 1 |   1   2   3   4   5   6   7
 2 |   2   4   6   8  10  12  14
 3 |   3   6   9  12  15  18  21
 4 |   4   8  12  16  20  24  28
 5 |   5  10  15  20  25  30  35
 6 |   6  12  18  24  30  36  42
 7 |   7  14  21  28  35  42  49
```

```
Please enter the table size: 1
       1
   +----
```

As seen, the table will change automatically depending on the input data by the user. Here is a description of how the program works:

- First, you must differentiate what is executed once in external loops from that which has been repeatedly done. Notice the column heading located across the top of the table outside all loops. Thus, the program implements a loop to print it once.
- The function to display the heading for the rows is spread across the execution of the external loop. The reason is that the heading for a particular row cannot be displayed until results for the previous row are printed.
- The statement to display the results:

```
print('{0:4}'.format(product), end='') # Display product
```

Right-justifies the product value inside the field that is four characters wide. This procedure will correctly arrange the columns inside the time's table.

- Within the nested loop, row belongs to the variable that controls the outer loop. The column will control the inner loop.
- The inner loop implements size times on every single iteration of the external loop. In other words, the innermost statement:

```
print('{0:4}'.format(product), end='')  # Display product
```

implement size x size times, one time for each product inside the table.

- The program will display a newline once it prints the details of every row. Therefore, all the values displayed in the inner column loop appear on the same line.

Nested loops are required when the iterative process needs to be repeated. In the time's table, the for loop displays the contents of every row and a surrounding for loop displays every row.

Nested loops increase efficiency in programming and some new programmers try to apply a nested loop where a single loop is the most preferred type. Before you start to determine a solution to a problem using a nested loop, make sure that there is no way you can apply a single loop. Keep in mind that nested loops aren't easy to write and when they aren't perfect for a given situation, they become less efficient than simple loops.

Sudden Loop Termination

In general, a while loop will run until it reaches that point when the condition is false. An executing program has to check this condition first before it can implement the statements inside the body of the loop. Next, it has to re-check the same condition only after running all statements within the body of the loop.

Typically, a while loop cannot suddenly exit its body even when the condition is false before it has executed all the statements inside the body. One reason why the while statement is designed to operate this way is that the programmer may want to run all the statements contained in the body as an invisible block. Despite this, there are times when it is important to suddenly terminate the body, or verify the condition from the middle of the loop.

Simply put, a while statement always verifies its condition at the top of the loop alone. It is not a matter of a while loop completing the operation immediately, the condition is true. Here is a program to illustrate this top-exit behavior:

```
x = 10
while x == 10:
print('First print statement in the while loop')
x = 5 # Condition no longer true; do we exit immediately?
print('Second print statement in the while loop')
```

Output

```
First print statement in the while loop
Second print statement in the while loop
```

Even if the condition that drives the loop execution changes inside the loop's body, the while statement cannot recheck the condition until it completes to execute statements inside the body.

There are cases where it is better to exit a loop from the center of the loop. This means you terminate the loop before all statements within the body finish executing. In other words, if a given condition is met in the body of the loop, end the loop instantly.

The same is true when it comes to for statement. There are instances where it is necessary to terminate the for a loop early. In this case, Python has a way to do that. And by applying the break statement, and continue statement, programmers have a lot of flexibility on their side.

Break Statement

As previously noted, sometimes, it is important to end the loop from the center of its body. This means you terminate the loop before completing executing statements inside the body. Therefore, when a specific condition is fulfilled inside the body of the loop, terminate the loop immediately. The "middle-exiting" requirement could be the same requirement that controls the while loop but it is not a must for it to be.

Python has the break statement that is used to run middle-exiting loop logic. The break statement affects the execution pattern of the break statement such that it will instantly exit from the loop's body.

The following program demonstrates the application of the break statement:

```
# Allow the user to enter a sequence of nonnegative
# numbers. The user ends the list with a negative
# number. At the end the sum of the nonnegative
# numbers entered is displayed. The program prints
# zero if the user provides no nonnegative numbers.
entry = 0 # Ensure the loop is entered
sum = 0 # Initialize sum
# Request input from the user
print("Enter numbers to sum, negative number ends list:")
while True: # Loop forever? Not really
entry = int(input()) # Get the value
if entry < 0: # Is number negative number?
break # If so, exit the loop
sum += entry # Add entry to running sum
print("Sum =", sum) # Display the sum
```

The condition of the ***while*** statement will always be true. Therefore, when the program executes, it is a must for it to start to implement the statements inside the ***while*** block at least once.

Since the condition of the ***while*** statement is a tautology, using the ***break*** statement is the only means to exit the loop. In this case, the break statement only implements once it verifies that the number entered by the user is negative. When the program comes across a ***break*** statement during its implementation, it jumps any statements that come after the body of the loop and terminates the loop immediately.

The reserved word ***break*** implies "break out of the loop." The location of the break statement in the previous example makes it hard to add a negative number to the variable sum.

Some designers of software programming advise programmers to limit the use of break statement in their programs because it strays from the normal loop control logic. Typically, each loop should contain a single entry point as well as a single exit point.

Still, some developers include the ***break*** statements inside the ***while*** statements where the condition for a ***while*** isn't a tautology. Including a break statement to this loop creates another exit point. Many programmers consider two exit points as acceptable, but having two break points in a single loop is dubious, and you should avoid this coding practice.

The break statement isn't necessary for complete control in a while loop. In other words, you can rewrite a Python program that has a break statement inside a while loop so that it can behave exactly but it doesn't include a ***break***.

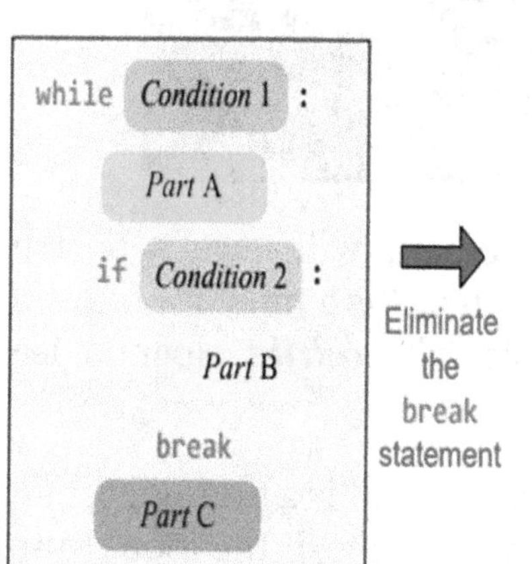

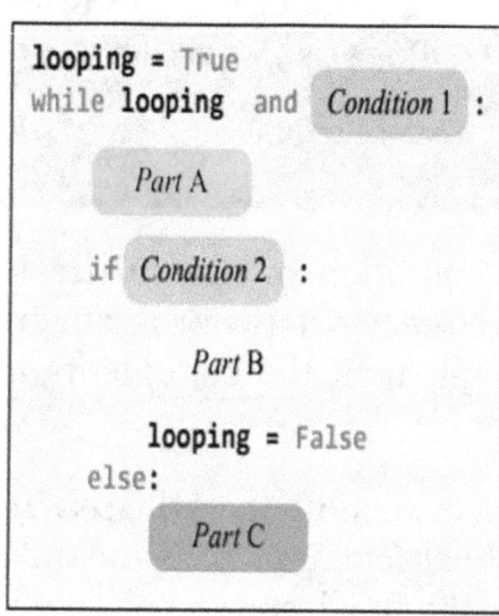

The left code illustrates a "while loop" that includes a "break statement." Towards the right, the loop is converted into a function equivalent that doesn't apply a break statement.

When you don't use a break version, then you have to consider the Boolean variable and the advanced state of the logic control loop. Also, this program without a break statement has additional overheads. For instance, it will consume more time and memory. However, the extra overhead is invisible. Even when it is insignificant, you need to note that it is more difficult to write this particular code. That is why a simple break statement can be a better control option.

Additionally, it is possible to include a break statement within a ***for*** loop. Here is an example of how you can let a break statement end a for loop.

```
word = input('Enter text (no X\'s, please): ')
vowel_count = 0
for c in word:
if c == 'A' or c == 'a' or c == 'E' or c == 'e' \
or c == 'I' or c == 'i' or c == 'O' or c == 'o':
print(c, ', ', sep='', end='') # Print the vowel
vowel_count += 1 # Count the vowel
elif c == 'X' or c =='x':
break
print(' (', vowel_count, ' vowels)', sep='')
```

If the program finds an X or x entered by the user, it will terminate from the loop suddenly. Take a look at this sample program.

```
Enter text (no X's, please): Mary had a lixtle lamb.
a, a, a, i,  (4 vowels)
```

This program will exit from the loop when it tries to execute x.

The ***break*** statement is crucial when instances arise that demand quick termination of the loop. In Python language, the ***for*** loop will function differently from the way a ***while*** loop operates. The ***for*** loop doesn't have an explicit condition that it verifies to proceed with the execution. You have to apply a break statement if you want to exit prematurely from a ***for*** loop before it has finished its iterations. The ***for*** loop is fixed loop, in this case, programmer can predict the number of iterations the loop will run. The ***break*** statement can destroy this predictability.

As a result, programmers prefer to use a break statement in place of ***for*** loops less often.

Continue Statement

When the execution of a program comes across a break statement within a loop, it jumps the remaining code within the body of the loop and skips the loop.

The ***continue*** statement resembles the break statement in many ways; the only distinction is that the continue statement doesn't really terminate the loop.

Continue statement jumps the remaining code inside the loop's body and instantly verifies the condition of the loop. In case the condition of the loop is true, the execution of the loop restarts at the top of the loop. This program demonstrates a ***continue*** statement in operation:

```
sum = 0
done = False
while not done:
val = int(input("Enter positive integer (999 quits):"))
if val < 0:
print("Negative value", val, "ignored")
continue # Skip rest of body for this iteration
if val != 999:
print("Tallying", val)
sum += val
else:
done = (val == 999) # 999 entry exits loop
print("sum =", sum)
```

Many programmers don't use the continue statement the same way they do with the break statement because it is easy to change a code that has a continue statement into one that doesn't have. The following program doesn't use a continue statement:

```
sum = 0
done = False
while not done:
val = int(input("Enter positive integer (999 quits):"))
if val < 0:
print("Negative value", val, "ignored")
else:
if val != 999:
print("Tallying", val)
sum += val
else:
done = (val == 999) # 999 entry exits loop
print("sum =", sum)
```

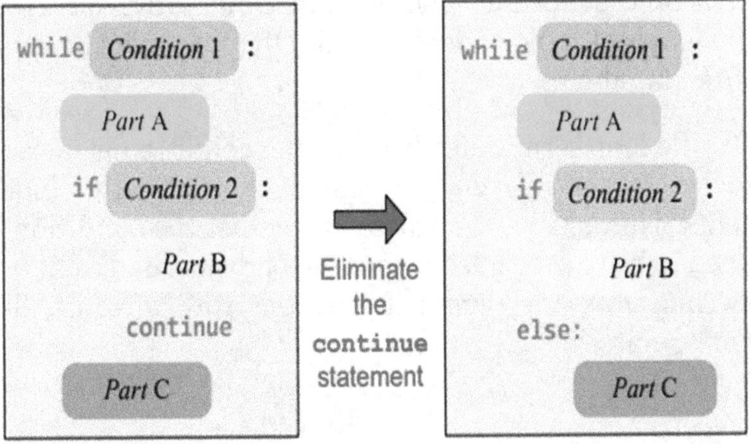

The left code features any loop that includes the continue statement. It is possible to change the code on the left by removing the continue statement. As demonstrated by the code on the right.

This change is quite easy compared to that of a break statement. And the reason for this simplicity is because the condition of the loop remains the same and no extra variable is required. The logic applied in the else version is not advanced than the continue version. Unlike the break statement discussed previously, there is no convincing reason to use a continue statement. There are moments when a programmer may insert a continue statement at the last minute to deal with an exceptional condition that went unattended. If loop's body is long, the programmer can include a conditional statement plus a continue at the top of the loop's body without handling the logic of the remaining loop. For that reason, the continue statement is a convenient choice for the developer.

While/Else and For/Else

Loops in python allow another optional ***else*** block. The else block in the form of a loop generates code to run when the loop terminates in the normal fashion. Put differently, the code inside the loop's else block doesn't run if the loop exits because of a ***break*** statement.

When a while loop terminates because the condition is false in the process of usual check, it's connected else block implements. This is true, regardless of whether the condition is determined to be true or false before the body has had a chance to run. This program demonstrates the way a while/else statement operates:

```
# Add five nonnegative numbers supplied by the user
count = sum = 0
print('Please provide five nonnegative numbers when prompted')
while count < 5:
# Get value from the user
val = float(input('Enter number: '))
if val < 0:
print('Negative numbers not acceptable! Terminating')
break
count += 1
sum += val
else:
print('Average =', sum/count)
```

In this program, once the user enters only nonnegative values, the program will evaluate the average of the entered values.

If the user fails to follow the instructions, the program will display a corrective action message but it will not try to evaluate the average.

```
Please provide five nonnegative numbers when prompted
Enter number: 23
Enter number: 12
Enter number: 14
Enter number: 10
Enter number: 11
Average = 14.0
```

It can appear natural to read the else keyword for the while statement like, "if no break," implies run the code inside the else block in case the program's execution within the while unit did not meet the break statement.

The else block isn't important. This program applies the if...else statement to accomplish the same effect.

```
# Add five nonnegative numbers supplied by the user
count = sum = 0
print('Please provide five nonnegative numbers when prompted')
while count < 5:
# Get value from the user
val = float(input('Enter number: '))
if val < 0:
break
count += 1
sum += val
if count < 5:
    print('Negative numbers not acceptable! Terminating')
else:
print('Average =', sum/count)
```

A for statement connected with an else block works the same way as the while/else statement. When this statement terminates because it has determined all values in a range or characters in the string, it implements the code found in the connected else block. When a for ...else block terminates prematurely after encountering a break statement, it will not implement the code inside the else block. The following program illustrates how for...else works:

```
word = input('Enter text (no X\'s, please): ')
vowel_count = 0
for c in word:
if c == 'A' or c == 'a' or c == 'E' or c == 'e' \
or c == 'I' or c == 'i' or c == 'O' or c == 'o':
print(c, ', ', sep='', end='') # Print the vowel
vowel_count += 1 # Count the vowel
elif c == 'X' or c =='x':
print('X not allowed')
break
else:
print(' (', vowel_count, ' vowels)', sep='')
```

Infinite Loops

For new programmers, infinite loop refers to one that runs a block of statement iteratively until the user forces the program to stop. As long as the flow of the program switches into the loop's body, it cannot escape.

In some cases, infinite loops occur because of design. For instance, a long-running server application like the web server may be required to check every time for incoming connections. The web server can accomplish this process using a loop that executes indefinitely. Unfortunately, new developers create infinite loops accidentally while coding and result in logic errors within their programs.

A deliberate infinite loop should be made public. For example:

```
while True:
# Do something forever. . .
```

In this code fragment, the Boolean Literal True will be true forever. So the only way to terminate the loop is to use a break statement. It is easy to create deliberate infinite loops. But accidental infinite loops are very popular but can be a huge mountain to climb for new developers.

To avoid creating infinite loops, you need to make sure that the loop contains specific features:

- The condition of the loop should not be a tautology. For example:

```
while i >= 1 or i <= 10:
# Block of code follows ...
```

The above statement will generate an infinite loop because any value selected for i will fulfill the condition. Probably the programmer wanted to use ***and*** rather than ***or*** to remain in the loop if i is in the range between 1-10.

- Initially, the while condition has to be true to access its body. The code inside the body must change program state in one way so that it can affect the result of the condition that has confirmed at every iteration. This always means that the body must change one of the variables applied in the condition. Finally, the variable takes a value that causes the condition to become false, and the loop exits.

Chapter 11: Tips to Learn Python Programming

We are happy that you have made up your mind to start the journey of mastering Python. One of the most common questions that new learners want to know is how to learn a given language.

Well, the first step in becoming a master in Python programming is to ensure that you know how to learn. Knowing how to learn is a vital skill in computer programming.

So why is it important for you to know how to learn? Simply put: language changes, new libraries are created, and new tools are released. Thus, if you know how to learn, it will be important to help you remain at par with these changes and become a successful developer.

This chapter will provide you with tips that will help you kick start your journey of becoming a master in python programming.

How to Make New Concepts Stick

Practice coding daily

Consistency is a key element when trying to learn anything new. Whether you want to learn how to drive a car, how to cook pizza, or even play basketball, you must be consistent. And learning a new language isn't an exception. You may not believe it but the muscle memory plays a huge role in programming. By coding daily, you will be boosting that muscle memory. Although this can be difficult in the first few weeks, you should try and begin with 25 minutes per day, and slowly increase the length of time each day.

Write something down

Concepts will not stick in your brain just by staring at them; you must have a pen and a notebook to take notes. Research indicates that taking notes by hand increases the level of retention. If you want to become a full-time Python developer, then you must take notes, and write down some lines of code.

Once you begin to work on small programs, writing by hand can assist you to know how to plan your code before you shift to the computer. This will help you save a lot of time, especially if you can write out the type of functions, variables, and classes you will need.

Don't be dull but be active

Whether you are learning how to debug an application or learning about Python lists, the Python shell should be your favorite tool. Use it to test out some Python codes and concept.

Give yourself a break

You know that work without play makes Jack a dull boy, so take breaks and allow the concepts to sink. Take a break of 25 minutes, then come back and resume your learning process. Breaks ensure that you have an efficient study session, especially when you are learning new information.

Breaks will be crucial when you start to debug your program. If you get a bug and you can't tell how to fix it, a break could answer to your problem. Step away from your computer and refresh yourself.

Maybe it could be a missing quotation mark that is preventing your program from running, and that break will make a difference.

Love to fix bugs

When it comes to hitting bugs, this is one thing that you will never miss if you begin to write advanced Python programs. Running into bugs is something that happens to everyone who codes. It doesn't matter which language you are using. Don't let bugs get the better of you. So you need to embrace any moment you encounter a bug and think of yourself as a master of solving bugs.

When you start to debug, ensure that you have a methodological strategy to assist you in identifying where things are going wrong. Scanning through your code by following the steps in which the program is implemented is a great way to debug. Once you identify the problem, then you can think of how to solve it.

Work with others

Surround yourself with people who are learning

While coding can appear as a solitary task, it really works well when you collaborate with others. It is very crucial that when you are learning how to program in Python that you have friends who are in the same boat as you. This will give you room to share amongst yourselves the tricks to help in learning.

Don't be scared if you don't have anyone that you can collaborate with. In fact, there are many ways to meet like-minded developers passionate about Python development. You can go to local events and peer to peer learning community for Python lovers and Meetups.

Teach

The best way to master something is to teach others. This is true when you are learning Python. There are different ways you can do this. For example, you can create blog posts that describe newly learned concepts, record videos where you explain something, or even talk to yourself. Each of these methods will solidify your knowledge and reveal any gaps in your understanding.

Try out pair programming

In this approach, two programmers work in a single workstation to finish a task. The two developers then switch tasks. One writes the code and the other one guides the process and reviews the code as it is being written. Switch tasks often to experience the benefit of both sides.

This technique has many advantages. For instance, you get the chance to have another person review your code and also see how the other person could be thinking about the problem. By getting exposed to numerous ideas and approaches of thinking will help you know how to create solutions to problems using Python.

Ask smart questions

You may have heard someone say that there is no bad question but in programming, it is possible to ask a bad question. When asking questions from someone who has very little knowledge or context of the problem you want to solve, it is advised to follow this format:

G: Give context on the area you want to solve.

O: Outline everything you have attempted to fix

O: Offer the best guess of what the problem could be.

D: Demonstrate what is happening

Asking a good question can save a lot of time. If you skip any of the following steps can lead to conflict because of the back-and-forth conversations. As a newbie, you want to ensure that you only ask good questions so that you can learn how to express your thought process. Also, the people who help you can be happy to assist you again.

Create something

Above all, you only learn by doing. Doing exercises will help you make important steps but building something will take you far.

Build anything

For new beginners, there are always small exercises that will boost your confidence in Python. Once you have a solid foundation on basic data structures, writing classes, and object-oriented programming, then you can begin to build something.

What you build is not as important as the method you use. The path of the building is what will help you learn the most. You can only learn a lot from reading Python books, articles, and courses. Most of your learning will originate from developing something. The problems you will solve will help you learn a lot.

If you find it hard to come up with a python practice project to work on, you can get started with the following:

- Dice roll simulator.
- Number guessing game.
- Simple calculator.
- Bitcoin price notification system

Participate in open source programs

In the open source system, you can access the source code of a software, and anyone can take part. Python has a lot of open-source projects that you can decide to contribute.

Besides that, many companies post open-source projects. In other words, you can contribute to the code written and generated by engineers working in some of these companies.

Conclusion

We have covered the basics of Python programming language. The constructs we have learned so far, such as loops, expressions, and conditions, should be enough to help you further your career in Python development. What we have covered is enough to help you understand Python examples.

Although not everything has been covered, we have tried to provide you with a refresher in Python that you can build on it to become an excellent programmer. Python is one of the top four widely used programming language. As it has increased in popularity, its main focus on the quality of code and readability, plus the associated impact on developer productivity, appears to have been the driving force to Python success.

If you experience difficulties with some of the concepts discussed in this book, it is good if you can explore other introductory resources to help you understand. Or you can even consult with an experienced Python developer.

In general, you should master the basics of python discussed inside this book, master the language syntax, and then start to deepen your knowledge on specific features of python. Keep in mind that great programmers don't stop learning. So make a point always to learn something new in Python every day.

CPSIA information can be obtained
at www.ICGtesting.com
Printed in the USA
LVHW080507100121
676040LV00001B/25